Florence Nightingale

The Lives and Careers of History's Most Influential Nurses

(The Famous Nurse Who Made Hospitals Safer and Saved Thousands of Lives)

Arthur Garret

Published By **Elena Holly**

Arthur Garret

Florence Nightingale: The Lives and Careers of History's Most Influential Nurses (The Famous Nurse Who Made Hospitals Safer and Saved Thousands of Lives)

ISBN 978-1-7780652-6-2

No part of this guidebook shall be reproduced in any form without permission in writing from the publisher except in the case of brief quotations embodied in critical articles or reviews.

Legal & Disclaimer

The information contained in this book is not designed to replace or take the place of any form of medicine or professional medical advice. The information in this book has been provided for educational & entertainment purposes only.

The information contained in this book has been compiled from sources deemed reliable, and it is accurate to the best of the Author's knowledge; however, the Author cannot guarantee its accuracy and validity and cannot be held liable for any errors or omissions. Changes are periodically made to this book. You must consult your doctor or get professional medical advice before using any of the suggested remedies, techniques, or information in this book.

Upon using the information contained in this book, you agree to hold harmless the Author from and against any damages, costs, and expenses, including any legal fees potentially resulting from the application of any of the information provided by this guide. This disclaimer applies to any damages or injury caused by the use and application, whether directly or indirectly, of any advice or information presented, whether for breach of contract, tort, negligence, personal injury, criminal intent, or under any other cause of action.

You agree to accept all risks of using the information presented inside this book. You need to consult a professional medical practitioner in order to ensure you are both able and healthy enough to participate in this program.

Table Of Contents

Chapter 1: Luxurious Refinement of the Best Type

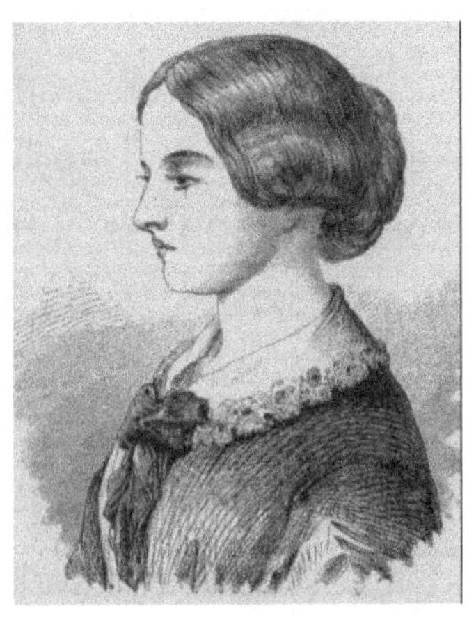

Young Florence

"Florence Nightingale come to be born in Florence, Italy, inside the year 1820, within the route of a wintry weather's sojourn of her dad and mom there. One of simplest daughters of wealthy mother and father, she have come to be introduced up in all the steeply-priced refinement of the high-quality sort of English home, inside the midst of a big and affectionate circle of relatives connection, in an surroundings enriched through manner of all the intellectual benefits and the happiness that such activities may additionally moreover need to keep. ... She end up a healthful little one, eager on a frolic, and no longer loose from unregenerate impulses in the direction of unsympathetic governesses, but, on the complete, extreme-minded, and a bit self-absorbed, with a unethical to introspection that now and again verged upon the morbid, and a dishonest to belittle herself and her powers, that arose in component out of a conscientious expertise of her very own shortcomings, and in element from a natural shyness, amounting nearly to self-attention. ... Mr. Nightingale held views at the better schooling of ladies that were a long way earlier of his time. He in my opinion supervised the training of his daughters, himself coaching them, as they grew older, modern languages and classics, European and Constitutional History, or maybe better arithmetic. They wrote essays and analyzed philosophical treatises, pursuing a good deal the identical route of examine, beneath his tutorship, as could be accompanied now for a college degree." - Mary Cowden Clarke, World-stated ladies: or, Types of womanly attributes of all lands and some time (1858)

"So in no manner lose an opportunity of urging a practical starting, however small, for it is exquisite how often in such subjects the mustard-seed germinates and roots itself." – Florence Nightingale

While there were many girls in the route of history who've accomplished awesome matters, few ever received the adulation each in existence and in loss of life that Florence Nightingale has enjoyed. Indeed, her very call is synonymous with no longer in fact an entire profession (and one of the first which a respectable lady have to pursue) but to any form of mild care given at any time. Much has been justly manufactured from her piety and the revel in that she have become known as with the aid of manner of God for a unique reason, and this in reality seems to be actual, specifically on the identical time as one appears at the unique situations that surrounded her begin and childhood.

Florence emerge as precise from start, clearly as became her call, for at the same time as many girls may later be named for her, she modified into named for the town wherein she have become born on May 12, 1820: Florence, Italy. To recognize how uncommon her name modified into, one best has to keep in mind that of her older sister, Frances Parthenope. In naming their daughters, William and Frances Nightingale set the degree for the uncommon way in which they may growth their high-quality children, especially in regard to their educations. William Nightingale have become a Unitarian and believed that women have to be informed in addition to men, so he took it upon himself to homeschool his daughters, giving them an education any guy of that era need to nicely envy. According to a 1858 biography of his more youthful daughter, Florence "is a younger woman of singular endowments, each natural and bought. She possesses a facts of the historic languages, and of the higher branches of mathematics; at the same time as her attainments in vast art work, science, and literature, are of no not unusual order. Her command of present day-day languages is large; and she or he speaks French, German, and Italian, fluently as her neighborhood English." Another biographer, writing only some years after her loss of existence, noted, "Florence modified into an ardent and laborious student, springing up often at four inside the morning to carry out her preparations, and, as Sir Edward Cook feedback, to her father's guidance in the ones processes she end up genuinely indebted for the intellectual hold close and energy of highbrow attention that high-quality her paintings in later lifestyles."

One of the Nightingale houses in England

Florence's sister

When in England, Florence divided her time among her wealthy dad and mom' u . S . A . Estates, wherein she grow to be apparently regarded even at a younger age for having a healing touch, which include as quick as bandaging the broken paw of an injured collie and nursing it back fitness to keep the dog from being placed down.

Not handiest had been the Nightingale daughters well-informed, they have been furthermore nicely travelled; even in advance than Florence went to the Crimea throughout the Crimean battle, she "visited and studied the numerous worldwide locations of Europe, and has ascended the Nile to its farthest cataract." The 1858 biography described, "In 1837, even as his greater youthful daughter changed into seventeen, Mr. Nightingale took his circle of relatives to the Continent, and eighteen pleasant months had been spent in leisurely journey thru France, Italy and Switzerland. Everywhere the remarkable social, creative, musical, literary and political circles had been open to them, and they entered heartily into the complicated overseas lifestyles about them. The tour ended with a wintry weather in Paris, in which, in the amazing salons in their buddies, the 2 charming ladies found themselves both appealing and attracted. Freed from the shyness that had afflicted her, Florence determined she had social gives of a excessive order, and confesses in her diary that the ultimate temptation she had to overcome, earlier than she became loose to interpret that insistent internal call, became a 'preference to shine in society.'"

Part of what attracted more youthful Florence to the Parisians changed into her relationship with Mary Clarke Mohl, a well-known hostess and Proto-feminist. Though married, Mohl lived her life in keeping with her private possibilities and insisted that girls need to do as they favored, with out regard to the regulations of guys and society. Mohl stimulated Florence and the 2 remained pals until Mohl's lack of existence some 40 years later.

Mohl

Florence's social targets quick proved inadequate, and "after their go back to England, and a brief London season...a revel in of the inadequacy of the social pleasures and home joys that surrounded her came upon her. It was to boom with the years, till, lengthy before she attained her freedom, she struggled closer to the regulations that certain her, with all of the restlessness of a caged chicken." Indeed, she later wrote that on February 7, 1837, "God called me to His employer."

During the Victorian Era, this sort of call would most probably be to non secular life as a nun, but this form of possibility supplied innumerable challenges to Nightingale, particularly her relationship at the side of her mother and father, to whom she have turn out to be very committed. On the best hand, her father, who had informed her and spent greater time together along with her than maximum men of his era spent with their younger sons a brilliant deal much less their daughters, have turn out to be a Unitarian, a broadly Protestant Church that eschewed all sorts of non secular professions. On the other hand, her mother, who had taught her from the cradle the significance of philanthropy and company to others, have grow to be a member of the Church of England, and whilst the latter had religious orders, they had been now not generally visible because of the fact the purview of the higher training. On top of this, Nightingale had no experience of a especially spiritual vocation but more one in every of devoting herself definitely to company to mankind, with none spiritual strings related.

Moreover, her mother and father, for all the liberality with which they raised her, had been now not prepared to appearance their younger daughter abandon a existence of fortune and simplicity for tough paintings. They, like many others of their situation, observed their baby's fervor as a passing segment, one from which she may be drawn and redirected. To that prevent, everyday with Eliza Pollard, "It turned into with an affectionate desire of distracting her from her tiresome cause, and with an entire loss of sympathy in her feeling, that her mom and sister deliberate and arranged numerous continental trips for her with congenial buddies. The wintry climate of 1847 was spent in Rome, at the side of her buddies the Bracebridges, who afterwards served at the side of her in the Crimea."

However, as is so frequently the case in such conditions, their efforts backfired, and "it changed into an eventful twelve months for the destiny of her choice in more than one appreciate. In Rome she met Sidney Herbert, and started that friendship with Lord Herbert, that became so fruitful in extremely good outcomes within the Crimea and after. And she became intimate with and studied the strategies of an Italian nursing sisterhood." Indeed, as Secretary at War in the path of the Crimean War, Herbert ought to show critical to Nightingale's destiny.

Herbert

Still decided to shop her from herself, Florence's circle of relatives sent her to Egypt and Greece with Charles and Selina Bracebridge within the wintry weather of 1849-50. Nightingale later wrote of the temples at Abu Simbel, "Sublime within the maximum fashion of highbrow splendor, mind with out try, with out struggling. I ought to no longer name it highbrow each, it's so really towards that of the Jupiter Capitolinus—it's far extra the beauty of the soul--no longer a feature is accurate but the entire effect is more expressive of spiritual grandeur than whatever I have to have imagined. It makes the impact upon one that lots of voices do, uniting in a single unanimous simultaneous feeling of enthusiasm or emotion, this is stated to triumph over the most powerful man. Yet the figures are anything but lovely...it is a new language to analyze and we have no language to unique it."

Holger Weinant's image of the temples at Abu Simbel

Naturally, there was loads more on Nightingale's mind than the splendor around right here; she also noticed the poverty and struggling the people in Egypt lived in. While near Cairo, she wrote to her sister about the decision she have been considering, telling her that "God called me within the morning and asked me could I do top for him by myself with out reputation." Pollard wrote, "It became on her manner lower decrease back to England from Greece, on July 31, 1850, that she first visited the Deaconesses Institute at Kaiserwerth on the Rhine. This have been the purpose of her dreams for the remaining six years, and over and over her hopes to look it had met with disappointment. It come to be a Protestant Sisterhood, prepared thru using Pastor Fliedner and his associate, for the care of the unwell horrible, and discharged prisoners, and for the education of orphans, along strains which appealed intensely to her. The deaconesses took no vows, but got here voluntarily, because of the truth they felt a vocation. She spent a fortnight inside the employer then, and decrease again the subsequent summer time (1851), the unfastened consent of her dad and mom having at very last been acquired, for three months' education. In the hard art work, lengthy hours, and ascetic simplicity of the existence, in addition to within the excessive-minded admonitions of the pastor, she took the internal maximum pleasure, and mentioned herself at ultimate "intensely happy." It modified right into a turning-factor in her career, for she got here to experience there that her lifestyles have become at final her very personal, and the time for indecision and yielding modified into beyond. There have been however issues and doubts at home, however she modified into not restless, but assured."

In 1858, writer Mary Cowden Clarke determined, "In 1851, even as the whole civilized global had a vacation at some point of the Great Exhibition, and had been engaged in parties of pleasure, Miss Nightingale end up inside the partitions of one of the German homes, or hospitals, for the care of the lost and infirm. At the Great Lutheran hospital, set up at Kaiserwerth, near Düsseldorf, on the Rhine, — an established order out of which no character is permitted to bypass to exercise as a nurse, besides after having lengthy gone via severe examination, — Miss Nightingale spent a few months in every day and nightly attendance on the ill and the miserable, accumulating enjoy in all the obligations and labours of girl ministration. The gentleman at the pinnacle of that repute quo, the Pastor Fhedner, asserted that considering he had been director of that employer, no one had ever surpassed so distinguished an exam, or demonstrated herself so very well mistress of all she needed to examine, as Miss Nightingale."

Chapter 2: A Really Passionate Altruism

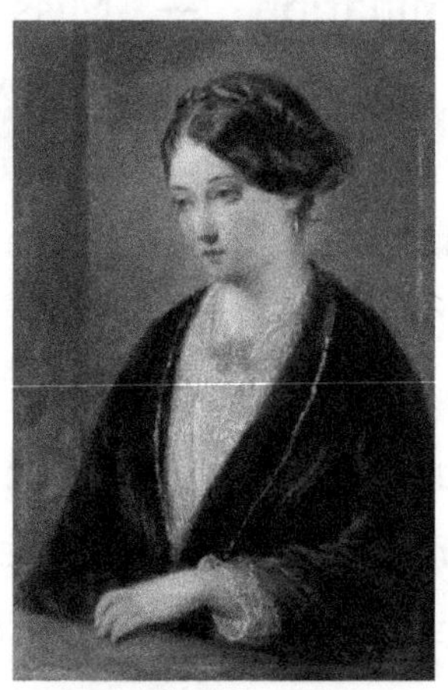

An 1840s portrait of Florence

"To understand the nature and the greatness of this a part of Miss Nightingale's achievement, that consisted in surmounting the limitations that lay within the manner of her schooling, one must undertaking oneself in creativeness into the age in which she lived...even as it turn out to be an unheard-of trouble for a cute and performed girl to do some element outside of the precincts of her home. Her mom and sister, affectionate as they had been, did now not even apprehend her impulse, and at the equal time as at remaining it formulated itself proper into a tremendous revel in of a vocation to take care of the unwell, because it did while she changed into twenty-five, they felt towards it a real disfavor. Nor can one blame them, remembering the low necessities of sanatorium lifestyles of in recent times and the degraded sort of nurse. She have become an affectionate and dutiful daughter, and yielded to her parents' desires for decades, doing her fantastic to be happy and to make others satisfied, in what emerge as to her a ceaseless round of trivia, and often struggling intensely from the texture of frustration of her better self. For, further to the truth that there were excellent powers of agency and execution fermenting in her thoughts, which at that factor had no outlet, and that she was swayed by using a really passionate altruism, Florence Nightingale changed into instead conscious, as lots in order each different saint in history, of a "call to be a saviour," as she expresses it extra than as soon as in her diaries." - Mary Cowden Clarke, World-noted girls: or, Types of womanly attributes of all lands and a while (1858)

"The international is located lower again thru the lack of lifestyles of every one which has to sacrifice the development of his or her brilliant objects to conventionality." – Florence Nightingale

Following her "graduation" from Kaiserwerth, Nightingale wrote her first ebook, The Institution of Kaiserswerth at the Rhine, for the Practical Training of Deaconesses, and so forth. Published anonymously in 1851, it installation her gift for agency, particularly because it finished to hospital therapy. Later, she studied with the Soeurs de l. A. Providence (Sisters of Providence) in Paris in February 1853, and a few months later she joined the personnel of the "Sick Governesses Home" on Harley

Street in London. By this time, Florence's parents had come to terms, as a minimum mainly, together in conjunction with her alternatives, so her father furnished her with the contemporary same of $sixty five,000 a twelve months, a sum that allowed her to live without a hassle on the identical time as working.

Despite being given that money, Florence became no longer one to throw coins about. In truth, she changed into relatively thrifty for one born to such wealth, and she or he became specially cautious with the cash of others. In early 1854, she wrote to one of her superiors, "I despatched Miss Varney off this morning with Miss Crossthwaite, having written to the Matron of the Institution that they have got been coming, and made all of the preparations in my electricity for their consolation. I despatched sandwiches and biscuits and a bit brandy with them for the adventure. Finding Miss Varny had no cash together collectively with her, I lent her £3 for her journey. Her medical man idea it pretty essential that every the young ladies have to pass first elegance and through the use of Express for goodbye a adventure - otherwise I have to fairly have regretted your being positioned to this prolonged charge - But he found no opportunity – This might not be vital on their go back."

According to Clarke, Nightingale changed into additionally a difficult employee who ---"emerge as seldom visible out of the partitions of the organisation; and the few pals whom she admitted, decided her inside the midst of nurses, letters, prescriptions, debts, and interruptions." This changed into difficult paintings, made greater so because of the manner in which she modified into raised. In truth, she later admitted, "As regards women...ordinary problems attend their admission [to the nursing profession]: however their eventual admixture to a amazing amount within the artwork is an essential characteristic of it. Obedience, concern, self-control, paintings understood as work, clinic service as implying masters, civil and medical, and a mistress, what provider manner, and abnegation of self, are subjects now not constantly easy to be learnt, understood, and faithfully acted upon, with the aid of the use of ladies. Yet they can not fail in overall performance of provider or propriety of conduct — propriety is a large word — without detrimental the work, and degrading their element. Their dismissal...need to constantly be extra tough, if not extra difficult than that of the opportunity nurses. It is probably better not to ask this detail ; to allow it come if it's going to look at, understand, and do what needs to be learnt, understood, and executed: if no longer, it's miles higher away. It appears to me, however I can be pretty flawed, that, within the beginning, many such parents will offer themselves, however few persevere; that in time a enough variety will form an important element of the art work; extra is not proper.

It appears to me important that ladies, as such, have to haven't any separate popularity; but have to be merged maximum of the pinnacle-nurses, with the aid of the use of a few issue call those are known as. Thus performance may be promoted, sundry topics can be checked, and the leaven would possibly flow into."

According to Sir Edward Cook, who knew Nightingale for my part, she knew the ones issues from private revel in. He later wrote, "Let people who reproach themselves for a desultoriness, apparently incurable, take coronary heart all all over again from the instance of Florence Nightingale! No self-reproach recurs more frequently in her personal outpourings right now, than that of irregularity or even sloth. She found it hard to upward thrust early within the morning; she prayed and wrestled to be added from desultory mind, from idle dreaming, from scrappiness in unselfish artwork. She wrestled, and she received."

When studying comments like this, it is straightforward to see Nightingale as some shape of far off saint, but people who knew her in her children portrayed her as honestly the opportunity. Photographs of her presently display that she changed into quite stunning, and Pollard said, "Florence Nightingale became no unhappy-eyed ascetic. We listen of her dealing with personal theatricals, mothering more youthful cousins, nursing maiden aunts, absorbed in house obligations obligations, sympathizing with the love affairs of buddies, and a bunch of diverse matters. ... She have become sought in marriage, extended and always, through manner of 1 with whom her very very very own coronary coronary coronary heart have become engaged. ... One of the maximum touching of her goodbye letters earlier than she left for the Crimea become from this buddy. 'You adopt this,' he wrote, 'while you can't adopt me!'" The man who made this assertion emerge as possibly Richard

Monckton Milnes, the First Baron of Houghton. He courted Nightingale for extra than nine years in advance than she in the end permit him go.

Milnes

While running in the health center, Nightingale commenced taking note of opinions of the terrible situations in British hospitals in the Crimea. War had broken out amongst England and Russia in early 1853, and the English were getting overwhelmed badly. Word also started out out to leak returned to London approximately situations some of the wounded infantrymen, inspiring a name for that some element must be completed.

Seeing an opportunity for each provider and journey, Nightingale gathered collectively 38 girls who had been willing to gain knowledge of as nurses. Among them emerge as her aunt, Mai Smith, and 15 Sisters of Charity, and after schooling them herself, she were given permission from Herbert to take them foreign places, first to Paris and then to the principle British camp within the Crimea. According to Clarke, "On the Friday following, Miss Nightingale and her partners embarked at Marseilles in the Vectis steamer; and, after a stormy passage, they reached Scutari at the 5th of November, without a doubt in advance than the wounded in the motion of Balaklava started out to acquire. Five rooms which have been set aside for wounded fashionable officers, have been happily unoccupied; and people were assigned to Miss Nightingale and her nurses..."

The Honorable Reverend Sydney Osborne wrote of Nightingale at this juncture, "Miss Nightingale in appearance, is without a doubt what you may expect in every other well-bred lady, who can also have seen, likely, as an possibility greater than thirty years of life: her manner and countenance are prepossessing, and this with out the ownership of extremely good splendor: it's far a face no longer with out issue forgotten, appealing in its smile, with an eye constant betokening fantastic self-ownership, and giving, at the identical time as she dreams, a quiet look of commercial enterprise enterprise self-discipline to every characteristic. Her famous demeanor is quiet, and as an possibility reserved: even though, I am an entire lot fallacious if she isn't proficient with a totally energetic experience of the ridiculous. In conversation, she speaks on subjects of business organization with a grave earnestness, one might also now not expect from her look. She has genuinely a thoughts disciplined to restrain below the thoughts of the motion of the immediately, each feeling that can intrude with it. She has skilled herself to command, and observed the fee of conciliation in the route of others, and constraint over herself I can conceive her to be a strict disciplinarian : she throws herself into a bit — as its Head — as such she is

aware about nicely how an awful lot success
ought to rely on literal obedience to her
every order. She seems to recognize
business enterprise very well."

Chapter 3: Benevolent Services

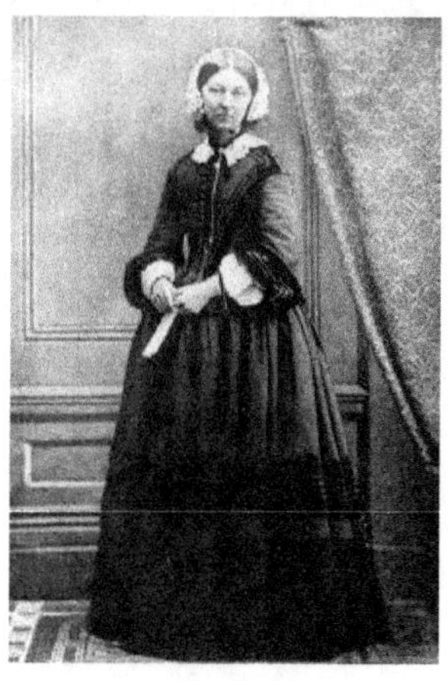

Florence within the 1850s

"During the primary months of her arrival, even as there has been nobody else to act, Miss Nightingale have end up the real purveyor of these enormous establishments — the hospitals at Scutari ; supplying what could not be obtained through the regular channels of the business enterprise, and, in particular from her kitchen, supplying comforts without which many a bad fellow ought to have died. Her name and benevolent services were the challenge of commonplace and thankful reward a number of the men inside the trenches; and the announcement modified into made, that she made the barrack health facility so comfortable, that the convalescents started out out to reveal a decided reluctance to move away it. Stores of shirts, flannels, socks, and 1000 different articles, which she and her nurses allocated; brandy, wine, and a selection of factors, required at a moment's phrase, and which can be procured from Miss Nightingale's quarters right away or tough formality, rendered her the digital purveyor for the whole of that length, in some unspecified time inside the future of which she modified into avowedly the character in whose retaining rested now not most effective the comfort, however the lifestyles of numerous thousand sick and wounded infantrymen." - Mary Cowden Clarke, World-stated girls: or, Types of womanly attributes of all lands and a long term (1858)

"The world is positioned again with the useful resource of using the dying of every person who has to sacrifice the improvement of his or her everyday items to conventionality." – Florence Nightingale

When Nightingale and her crew of nurses arrived at Selimiye Barracks in November 1854, they short realized they had their art work reduce out for them. For one aspect, maximum of these sick and injured in no way made it into the hospital proper however were as an alternative saved outdoor in tents. In February 1855, The Times referred to, "It appears to us, upon this assertion of facts, that the sanatorium accommodation in the mission for the ill and wounded has been very insufficient. The nature of this accommodations become, in our opinion, entirely incorrect for the treatment of the ill and wounded in wintry weather. Even the most comfortable marquee isn't unfastened from objection for the form of purpose; but bell-tents, as well from the materials of which they will be made as from their form and duration, are distinctly unwell tailor-made for medical institution purposes. They aren't continuously wind or water-tight, and that they do now not admit of greater than three or 4 stretchers or some different form of bedstead being applied in them. The quantity similarly to the first-rate of sanatorium inns changed into in our opinion inadequate."

Moreover, because the men have been spread out, the scientific medical doctors needed to paintings even greater tough than ordinary, on the aspect of taking walks through dust to get to each man or organization of fellows. According to the identical Times article, "In numerous instances we determined that maximum of the unwell had been dealt with of their private tents, for need of room in the sanatorium tents or marquees of their regiments. Although all of the men who've been at the ill listing did now not constantly require admission into hospital, we've got motive to agree with that a full-size quantity of these defined as attending health center had been now not admitted into it sincerely because of the fact there was no room for them. In the 88th Regiment, of the one hundred and twenty guys at the sick listing at the day of our go to 24 or 25 on my own had been in clinic, but more than double that variety, we were assured with the aid of way of the healthcare professional, wanted sanatorium accommodation. On the day of our go to to the sector clinic of the Sappers and Miners, the scientific professional in price informed us that he had 14 patients whom he became very desirous of stepping into the sanatorium marquee, but that he became now not capable to perform that from want of room."

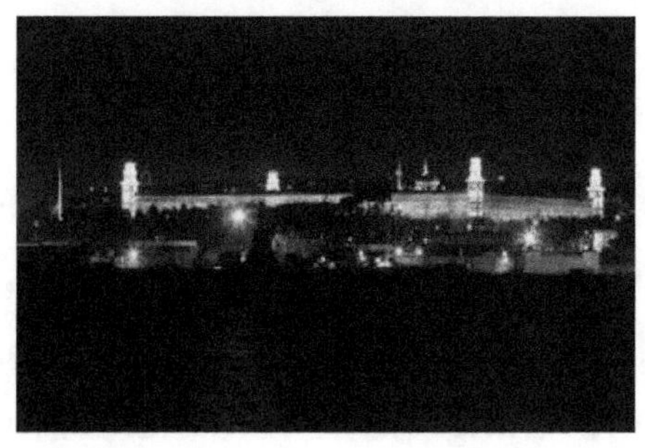

Selimiye Barracks

On top of that, Clarke referred to in 1858, "The issues of Miss Nightingale's assignment were not great those arising out of its very own appertaining perils and sacrifices, and people which resulted from respectable mismanagement; but she encountered a brilliant deal competition springing from expert prejudices and jealousies. On their first arriving, up to now from being welcomed, the appearance of the nurses became appeared upon as an evil, resented as an interference, and treated with tacit, if not open discountenance. At the remarkable, they have been tolerated, not advocated. Cabals had been got up, sick-feeling fostered, party versions disseminated and fomented. Passive resistance in each shape was resorted to, to prevent the installing of the nurses within the military hospitals. Against all this, now not some thing however the tremendous tact, firmness, and suitable enjoy of Miss Nightingale want to have prevailed. Having' proved herself a full of life reformer of sanatorium misrule, she had to stumble upon the tacit competition of almost all the vital clinical officers: her nurses have been sparingly resorted to, even inside the Barrack Hospital, at the identical time as inside the General Hospital, — the top-quarters of one of the chief medical government — she held a totally insecure footing."

Despite the issues, the British government's response to the contemporary-day complaints end up nothing brief of brilliant. It straight away contacted Isambard Kingdom Brunel, simply one in every of its most well-known and modern architects, and commissioned him to build a prefabricated form that might be constructed in England, disassembled, and shipped to the Crimea, wherein it could be rebuilt as a medical institution. Brunel jumped at the challenge and in the long run constructed Renkioi Hospital. Meticulous in detail, he wrote in September 1855, "The manner of landing with no trouble in all weathers have become made through using me one of the crucial situations of an amazing net website online and I directed that the situation of the prevailing winds being exactly opposite in Summer and Winter should be attended to - the website determined on gives this benefit to the fullest quantity being among bays with opposite exposures - and each shore at a very brief distance from the centre of the houses - The Jetty which may generally be in smooth water in some unspecified time in the future of the Summer end up first installed hand however this could very frequently be quite inaccessible within the course of the Winter - whilst within the period in-between the north east bay in which the second one Jetty have come to be to be located can be quite clean - I shall sense obliged therefore if you may authorise me to have this one proceeded with so that it may be entire earlier than the South and South West winds begin to blow." When completed, Renkioi have become the pinnacle-rated military medical institution inside the area and had 10% the loss of life fee of Scutari.

Brunel

Renkioi

Then there was the problem of number one belongings, which include beds for those struggling. While a number of the guys had beds, more lay on pallets at the floor. According to The Times, "We located a elegant want of bedsteads, stretchers, and every exclusive technique of raising the men above the ground. Even of the small deliver of Smith's and Clarke's stretchers on the disposal of the surgeons only a element turned into used, owing in element to the inadequate wide sort of marquees and tents available for health facility features, and in component to the incompleteness of the stretchers, many of that have been without legs on the transverse bars, which maintain them stretched. With a few uncommon exceptions, the guys have been with out mattresses or paliasses. They lay, in massive, on a blanket stretched over water-dock or rush-mat. In one case, underwood have come to be located below them. In another, the health care expert had unfold white marl over the floor. We observed no bolsters or pillows; the affected character's knapsack in widespread served for this cause. The supply of blankets have become in some times sufficient; but the guys have been frequently restricted to their location allowance. This changed into in a few times, a single blanket, for however the truth that a second have been typically allocated toward the middle of December, as we had been knowledgeable, this distribution turn out to be never favored. We did now not see a sheet in the camp."

An 1856 example depicting wounded soldiers and their situations

Not exceedingly given the technology, there has been almost no provision for sanitation, so those men not able to get outdoor to relieve themselves were regularly left in their very own dust. The reporter determined, "The deliver of medical institution utensils, additionally, seems to us to had been an extended manner too limited, at the same time as regard is paid to the range of unwell, and the general court instances, - diarrhoea and dysentery. Mr. Jenner knowledgeable us that he had no longer, at the day even as we examined him (January tenth), a unmarried urinal, bed-pan, or near-stool whole. He said that he had plenty of frames, but that the pans had no longer reached him. He additionally said that he had often been obliged to refuse requisitions for such subjects to regiments, specially currently. We determined, but, in his save loads of frames and steel vessels, which, even though no longer destined for this reason, spoke back for completing the item in query."

In fact, sanitation became considered certainly one of Nightingale's most priorities, and in a worldwide that had no knowledge of bacteria or germs, she however believed that cleanliness emerge as important to decreasing demise from infection. She insisted that each one those nursing below her route frequently wash their palms, and he or she or he moreover installation a wash residence, in which guys were assigned to launder sheets and clothing, consequently putting off the unfold of pathogens among patients. Much of the easy bedding and apparel the men had to trade into turn out to be provided because of charge range raised following the object within the Times.

In spite of Nightingale's wonderful efforts, more than 4,000 men misplaced their lives within the Scutari clinic in the path of her first wintry climate there, ninety% to illness in preference to wounds. Nightingale pleaded over and over to have the sewers repaired, but no one changed into dispatched to do this till March 1855. Once the sewers have been flushed out and repaired, the loss of life charge plummeted. Nightingale herself later wrote, "The cut price inside the mortality, after the Sanitary works were started, is maximum putting, and it falls in the long run to a good deal less than a 6th part of what it have emerge as on the equal time because the Barrack and General Hospitals were occupied together in October 1854, and to a 19th part of what it have turn out to be in February 1855. Our General Hospitals have been so deplorably mismanaged in all our wars that the question has been raised as to whether or not it might now not be higher to do without them altogether. The revel in of Scutari proves that General Hospitals may additionally moreover become pest-houses from neglect about, or may be made as healthful as every different houses." Indeed, clearly the lack of existence price plummeted from 42% to 2% after those measures were introduced.

Illustrations from the 1850s depicting Florence in Scutari clinic

In addition to sanitation, one of the maximum pressing problems, and the simplest that Nightingale first have turn out to be her hobby to, modified into the pleasant of nursing care the men have been receiving. This art work grow to be achieved no longer thru education people but through guys pulled from the ranks for the reason. Like maximum men of their era, they knew little to now not something approximately cooking, cleaning or nursing everybody, a extremely good deal much less the ones substantially unwell or badly injured. The Times article stated, "The orderlies have in component of numbers been commonly amply enough. In every particular respect, but, besides that of mere numbers, we regard this department of the health facility issuer as maximum unsatisfactory. The orderlies are drawn from the ranks, with none regard to their flair or their inclination for the employment, and are via and big men whose prone charter unfits them for the hardships of a marketing and marketing campaign, or convalescents who've not sufficiently recovered their health to go again to lively provider. The obligations of an sanatorium orderly are frequently distasteful to them; and the low charge of pay, 4d a day, isn't always sufficient inducement to them to conquer their repugnance. They are also at risk of be despatched back to their regiments, and their locations are then filled by means of men of the identical character, with out the gain of the enjoy which their predecessors obtained. We have to upload, that the overall conduct of our infantrymen do not drastically qualify them for a situation requiring brilliant balance of conduct; and from the rank of lifestyles to which they belong, and the terms of intimacy which glaringly subsist between themselves and their patients, they've got in no way the authority to prevent, (seldom the inclination to document) any irregularities which can also additionally come under their phrase. The ward-masters and assistant ward-masters are normally smart and decent non-commissioned officers; however they do now not possess that diploma of revel in in the obligations of their place of job which ought, in our opinion, to be an critical state of affairs to their employment inside the type of functionality in our army hospitals. The chefs also are soldiers; and regardless of the reality that they'll be useful as assistants, we count on that they're but indifferently acquainted with the unusual fashion of cooking required in hospitals."

Moccasins and different gadgets utilized by Nightingale inside the Crimea

Supplies endured to be hard to get during the struggle, and at the same time as late as April 1856, after the Treaty of Paris had already ended the battle, Nightingale turned into nevertheless begging for materials. At this time, she wrote, "May I ask whether or not or not it'd be viable to borrow or to buy 6 bottles Tincture of Myrrh (if four oz. Bottles) from the Medical Stores, changing them in any manner you shall direct, each in cash or in kind? I should not make this request had I no longer decided upon enquiry that the object is not available nearer than Constantinople - in any other case than from the Govt. Stores."

The first generation of nurses, jogging below Nightingale's supervision, spent as lots in their time on "domestic obligations" duties as they did palms-on nursing. Among their most pressing obligations grow to be cooking, as Nightingale knew all too properly the significance of particular food for those searching for to recover from any contamination. Though she had little expertise of the modern technological know-how of vitamins, she had long beyond along with her mom commonly to visit the in negative fitness and had seen her provide the patient some pork broth to drink. Using this idea, Nightingale ordered that her nurses speedy set up kitchens and begin producing the high-quality food they may for his or her sufferers. Clarke later advised, "In ten days after their arrival, Miss Nightingale and her assistants prepared up a kind of impromptu kitchen; and from this all of sudden built beneficial useful resource 8 hundred men had been each day provided with their respective requisite portions of properly cooked food, except red meat-tea in abundance. They who are familiar with the plan of cookery pursued in barracks, in which all a business enterprise's meat and veggies are boiled in a unmarried copper, the quantities belonging to messes being stored in separate nets, will comprehend how that meals is possibly to healthful the sickly urge for food of a fevered affected man or woman, and the manner beneficial a device which provided the needful light weight loss plan organized with due quickness as well as nicety, might be in health facility treatment. This have become effected through Miss Nightingale's kitchen, even in its early operation; and it in the end attained a diploma of excellence green of big benefit scarcely to be expected via the ones unacquainted with the importance of such details."

Based on her research in the Crimea and a few different vicinity, Nightingale herself stated, "Every cautious observer of the ill will agree on this, that thousands of patients are every year starved inside the midst of hundreds, from need of hobby to the strategies which on my own make it viable for them to take food. This need of interest is as brilliant in folks that urge upon the sick to do what is quite no longer viable to them, as in the unwell themselves who will now not take some time to do what's perfectly possible to them. For example, to the large majority of very prone sufferers it's miles quite impossible to take any solid food in advance than 11 A. M, nor then, if their power continues to be further exhausted by way of fasting till that hour. For willing sufferers have generally feverish nights, and, within the morning, dry mouths; and, if they may consume with the ones dry mouths, it might be the more excessive for them. A spoonful of red meat-tea, of arrowroot and wine, of egg turn, each hour, will provide them the needful nourishment, and save you them from being too much exhausted to take at a later hour the sturdy food, that's crucial for their recovery."

The nurses were additionally predicted to spend a large part of their "free time" sewing, thinking about that there had been few synthetic products designed especially for annoying for the unwell. Clarke talked about, "In what is probably referred to as 'house-preserving obligations,' she showed womanly accomplishment, no loads less than tremendous judgment. When the nurses were now not needed at the bedsides of the ill and wounded, they have been hired by using her in making up requisite articles of bedding, and surgical necessities, — together with stump pillows for amputation instances." The rate in their work became quick recognized thru the use of those at the the the front, as indicated via manner of one reporter: "Wherever there can be illness in its most volatile shape and the hand of the spoiler distressingly nigh, there may be that incomparable girl sure to be seen; her benignant presence is a strength for proper comfort, even amid the struggles of expiring nature. She is a 'ministering angel,' without any exaggeration, within the ones hospitals: and as her slender form glides quietly along each hall, every terrible fellow's face softens with gratitude on the sight of her. When all of the scientific officials have retired for the night, and silence and darkness have settled down upon those miles of prostrate sick, she may be observed on my own, with a piece lamp in her hand, making her solitary rounds. ... With the coronary coronary heart of a actual girl, and the manners of a lady, completed and sensitive beyond most of her intercourse, she combines a shocking calmness of judgment and promptitude and choice of man or woman. I with a bit of luck assert, that, however for Miss Nightingale, the humans of England should scarcely, with all their solicitude, were spared the additional pang of information, which they must have completed, in the long run, that then squaddies, even in medical institution, had observed scanty stable haven and remedy from the tremendous miseries with which this battle has hitherto been attended."

Articles like these unfold phrase about the paintings being accomplished via Nightingale and her nurses, and greater younger women started out begging their mother and father to be allowed to visit the Crimea and nurse. Likewise, they wrote to Nightingale in hopes of being familiar for training. For example, in February 1855, Emily Slesson wrote a letter asking for to be traditional: "I am very stressful to exit to assist both Miss Nightingale or Miss Stanley. I am very strong and could stand a terrific quantity of labor and fatigue. Twenty six and a half of years old searching rather older I think. My tremendous fear is that I am too past due in making use of to be sent out however in case greater nurses are preferred I accept as true with I is probably allowed to serve. Would you Madam be so very kind as to permit me realise if there may be any threat of my being able to go out? I expect I might also say I feel effective of being capable of finance myself very useful having tendencies of strength and nerve."

From the begin, Nightingale agreed to honestly take shipping of nurses with out regard to their spiritual records, a choice that irritated many inside the Church of England. In December 1854, Elizabeth Herbert wrote a letter defensive her buddy: "It is melancholy to count on that in Christian England nobody can adopt some thing with out the maximum uncharitable and sectarian attacks; and, had you no longer cautioned me so, I have to scarcely have believed that a clergyman of the Established Church could have been the mouthpiece of slander. Miss Nightingale is a member of the Established Church of England, and what's referred to as alternatively Low Church. But ever due to the fact she went to Scutari, her religious opinion and character had been assailed on all factors: — one character writes to upbraid us for having sent her, 'know-how she is a Unitarian;' any other, 'that she is a Roman Catholic,' and so forth. It is a merciless return to make toward one to whom England owes plenty. As to the charge of no Protestant nurses being sent, the subjoined listing will persuade you of its fallacy. We made no variations of creed; all and sundry who became a tremendous and skillful nurse, and understood the exercising in surgical wards, changed into regular, provided, of direction, that we had their friends' consent, and that in one of a kind respects, as a ways as we may additionally need to pick, they had been of unexceptionable person. A massive a part of the wounded being Roman Catholics, we commonplace the services of a number of the Sisters of Charity from St. Stephen's Hospital, Dublin." Herbert's husband wrote, "I endure in mind an exceptional solution being given to a query of this kind via an Irish clergyman, who even as he became asked to what sect Miss Nightingale belonged, replied: ' She belongs to a sect which alas is a completely uncommon one — the sect of the Good Samaritans.' "

Osborne, himself a minister within the Church of England, also defended her: "I found her myself to be in her each word and motion a Christian; I notion this pretty enough. It ought to were in my view the most cruel impertinence, to scrutinize her phrases and acts, to find out to which of the severa bodies of real Christians she belonged. I even have conversed in conjunction with her several instances at the deaths of those, who I had visited ministerially inside the hospitals, with whom she had been once they died. I in no manner heard one phrase from her lips that couldn't were clearly what I should have anticipated from the lips of folks that I actually have diagnosed to be the maximum expert and religious of our not unusual faith. Her art work need to answer for her religion; at least none ought to dare to call that faith in question, in opposition to such paintings, on grounds so susceptible and trivial as those I have seen suggested. That she has been in addition kind and aware of fellows of each creed; that she should easy the pillow and supply water to a lack of existence fellow-creature who could possibly very own no creed, I have no doubt; all honour to her that she does enjoy, that hers is the Samaritan's — not the Pharisee's work. If there can be blame in seeking out a Roman Catholic Priest to attend a loss of life Romanist, permit me percentage it along side her — I did it over and over."

Nightingale's willingness to artwork with Catholics extended a long way beyond the battlefield. In fact, she later despatched a big donation to Abbe Legendre, the fundraiser for the "Ceuvre de Notre Dame D'Orient," a shape of recuperation center for wound squaddies located in France. When sending the cash, she wrote, "I enjoy the warmest sympathy with you within the touching object of your art work, and I am satisfied to sign up for in it to the confined volume which my very private engagements allow. I obtained, too, from the remarkable religious women who were related to the French military within the East, so many tokens in their friendship, — they gave me their assist with such complete self-denial, and lightened my difficult project within the hospitals with masses devotedness, that I shall continuously searching out any opportunity of displaying my gratitude to France, and to her brave children, whom I have been taught by using using those girls to love and understand."

Once "on the grounds," the younger ladies who got here to nurse soldiers in the Crimea positioned a international very particular than the simplest that they'd left inside the decrease back of, or sincerely had ever expert and prepared for. Far eliminated from the familiarity and appropriately of home, they had to undergo the bodily and emotional toll their paintings took on them each day. One woman wrote, "I apprehend no longer what sight is maximum coronary heart-rending; to witness fantastic-searching, strong greater youthful men worn down with the beneficial resource of exhaustion, and sinking underneath it, or others coming in fearfully wounded. The whole of the day before today emerge as spent in sewing guys's mattresses together; then in washing and supporting the surgeons to get dressed their wounds; and seeing the awful fellows made as cushty as their circumstances may also need to admit of after five days' confinement on board ship, inside the route of which their wounds were not dressed. Out of the 4 wards devoted to my charge, 11 men died in the night time, honestly from exhaustion; which, humanly speaking, could have been stopped, need to I simply have laid my arms upon such nourishment as I understand they must have had."

One of the most coronary heart wrenching responsibilities for Nightingale and the others become writing letters of condolence to the households of the men they had nursed. Officers would probable usually write letters informing women or mother and father of the lack of a husband or son, however because of the fact they had to write such a lot of, those notes were commonly quick and mainly bloodless. Those who wanted to realise greater about their loved one's final hours sought a female's opinion, and Nightingale hardly ever disillusioned. She modified into furthermore sensible and careful to ensure that the households knew to whom they want to follow for in addition help. Her letter to Mrs. Laurence of South Shields is an wonderful example of this shape of missives, despite the fact that in this example the spouse had now not yet acquired the tragic information:

"Scutari Barrack Hospital, fifth March, 1856.

"Dear Mrs. Laurence, — I even have come to be alternatively grieved to attain your letter; because I absolutely have handiest sad information to offer you in move lower back. Alas! Within the terrible time we had final year, whilst we out of place from seventy to eighty guys in step with day in these hospitals by myself, many widows needed to undergo together with you; and your husband, I regret to say, grow to be some of the quantity. He died in this medical institution, February 20th, 1855, truly at the time on the identical time as our mortality reached its pinnacle of fever and dysentery; and on that day we buried eighty men. In order that I might be positive that there has been no mistake within the name, I wrote as a great deal as the colonel of his regiment, who confirms the statistics within the be aware I enclose ; and in spite of the truth that he is wrong in the excellent date of your husband's dying, there can be no mistake, lamentably ! Within the reality. I preferred to get this respond earlier than I wrote to you. Your husband's stability due to him emerge as £1. 2. Four^, which changed into remitted home to the Secretary of War, September 25th, 1855, from whom, you could have it on software application. As you've got got been no longer aware about being a widow, you're, of route, not in receipt of any allowance as a widow. You want to, therefore, make software program program to Colonel Lefroy, R. A., Hon. Secretary of the Patriotic Fund, sixteen a, Great George Street, Westminster, London. I enclose the crucial papers so that you can pinnacle off. Your colonel's letter may be enough evidence of your husband's lack of existence. I enclose it for the purpose. You will u . S . All info about your youngsters. Yom* minister will permit you to fill it up. I am very sorry for you and your problem. Should you have any difficulty about the Patriotic Fund, you may rent this letter, a good manner to be sufficient evidence which will produce of your being a widow. With sincere sympathy in your incredible loss, I live, yours virtually, Florence Nightingale."

Given all the boundaries, it's sincere to say that Nightingale and the nurses installation one of the most terrific bureaucratic turnarounds in facts. Within only a few short months, the nurses started out to make a difference, and The Times article concluded, "Besides the above health facility attendants, we need to word the staff of nurses under the superintendence of Miss Nightingale. That female arrived at Scutari at the 4th November, accompanied thru thirty-eight nurses. These are employed to attend to such instances because the scientific officers in charge, and the frame of human beings surgeons in their divisions, concur in considering times requiring such attendance. They are hired especially, regular with Miss Nightingale's evidence, some of the wounded, the operation times, and the intense medical instances. Their obligations consist, in surgical cases, in washing, and making ready for the morning visits of the medical officer, such wounds as they're directed via that officer to cope with on this manner; to attend upon him in dressing the injuries; and to get maintain of, and take to Miss Nightingale, his tips as to weight loss plan, drink, and clinical comforts. In surgical instances, a hall and wards are generally assigned to 4 nurses. In clinical instances, their obligations consist in dressing terrible sores, due to the truth the meals of the sufferers is nicely cooked and properly administered, and that cleanliness, every of the wards and of the person, is attended to. We have reason to consider that the offerings of these health center attendants have been highly precious."

In spite of criticisms that might be despatched her way, Nightingale's reviews remained an entire lot in call for. In March 1855, she wrote to Dr. Taylor of the L.T.C. Hospital regarding his efforts to enhance and standardize hospital care: "I want to be very happy, if I have to, to provide any assist, but humble, if you may be given it, for your plans. The best seems to be that of the 'Hospital Kit' for the guys, & of the Infirmary for the women. ... Lord Panmure acceded to the 'Hospital Kit' plan a few months ago, and knowledgeable me that it must be finished right away. I consequently end that I am appearing in conformity with the War Minister's plans in putting at your disposal that part of the 'Free Gifts' (for the use of the War Hospitals) which has returned domestic, & which I informed the War Department I need to destine to this reason & in filling up the deficiencies myself. ... As it's miles important that the issue must be accomplished as quietly as feasible, I will ask you to educate me a manner to retain. Whether I need to ship you an Inventory of what I sincerely have or whether or not you need to deliver me one of what you want. I will visit Lord Panmure...to settle the problem if you recommend it. It movements me that Fort Pitt is a fantastic location to begin because it ought to have room for Pack Stores."

Having dealt with the problem of the soldier's materials, Nightingale raised her worries approximately the topic that might consume lots of the rest of her existence: the nursing care of girls and children. She wrote, "Would you be kind sufficient to area the accompanying cheque at the disposal of the Female Hospital? I actually have concept a good deal near Soldiers' Wives, for the motive that what you counseled me & what I surely have seen. I actually have no longer forgotten your type invitation to go to Fort Pitt once more - which I shall gladly do.... I want not remind you of what you probable apprehend already. That I even have heard sufficient of "ostentatious & useless benevolence" to be conscious that, even have been I not a girl, it is of the very notable importance for me that every one subjects want to be carried out quietly."

This remaining sentence is interesting to contemplate, for it gives a huge perception into Nightingale's individual and methods. She have been hailed greater than as soon as as a feminist, and praised for the art work she did to allow girls to have careers outdoor the house. However, she emerge as never, it seems, as enamored of the hazard for equality as she became the danger to serve. This is well consistent with each her social and non secular upbringing. It moreover demonstrates her know-how, in that she knew the manner to paintings inside the Victorian system wherein she lived to get things finished. Thus, changed into she able to maintain such recognize, even the various maximum instructions, that Queen Victoria herself commemorated Nightingale with "a jewel, the format of which changed into even greater precious, in its lovely emblematic importance, than even the pricey gems that composed its adornment." According to Clarke, "It is defined as being long-established of a St.

George's cross, in ruby-purple teeth, on a white discipline, representing England. This is encircled via the use of a black band, typlifying the workplace of charity, on this is inscribed a golden legend, 'Blessed are the merciful.' The letters 'V. E.' surmounted through a crown in diamonds, are inspired upon the centre of the St. George's Cross, from which emanate rays of gold. Wide-spreading branches of palm in vibrant green tooth, tipped with gold, shape a framework for the guard, their stems being banded with a riband of blue teeth, inscribed with the phrase, ' Crimea.' At the pinnacle 3 top notch stars of diamonds illustrate the idea of the moderate of Heaven shed upon labours of Mercy, Peace, and Charity. On the once more of the jewel is an inscription written through manner of her Majesty, recording it to be a gift in reminiscence of services rendered to her courageous navy with the useful resource of Miss Nightingale."

Along with the winning came a personal phrase written through the Queen herself: "I desire Miss Nightingale and the women may additionally inform the ones horrible noble, wounded, and ill guys that no man or woman takes a hotter interest, or feels more for their sufferings, or admires their braveness and heroism more than their queen; day and night time time she thinks of her loved troops."

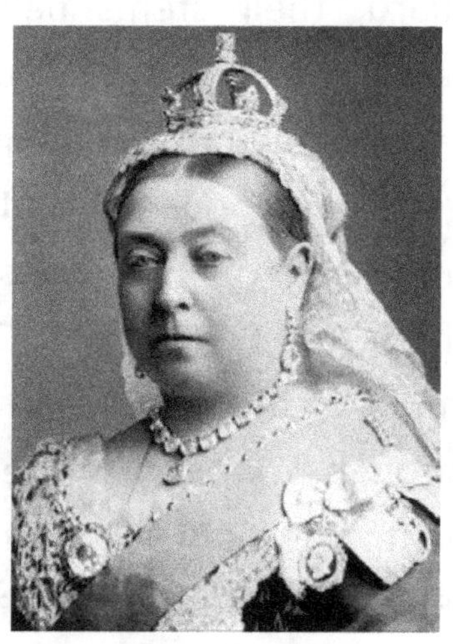

A print of the jewel presented to Florence
thru Queen Victoria

67

Queen Victoria

Chapter 4: Her Great Power

"Possessing the first-rate belief of the pathetic in existence which her entire profession publicizes her to have, — it would had been a illness in her nature, — nay, a lack of the complete feeling for pathos itself — had she now not betrayed a capability for receiving humorous impressions. Humour and pathos are so nearly allied, in their deliver in the human coronary coronary coronary heart, — so mingled in the ones recesses whence spring human tears at the contact of sympathy, that scarcely any being deeply laid low with mournful emotion, can stay insensible to the eager enchantment this is living in a ridiculous idea. Shakespeare, — who comprehended to perfection every impulse of humanity — gives multitudinous illustrations of this close to consociation of a experience of pathos and a experience of humour in the greatest natures. That particular characteristic chronicled via Mr. Osborne in his private description of Miss

Nightingale, is just the notable factor — to our creativeness — that crowns her admirable functions. It accords with an intensely stunning account of her, that grow to be elated with the useful resource of Mr. Sydney Herbert at a public assembly, convened in Miss Nightingale's honour. He stated, an anecdote had in recent times been despatched to him with the aid of using a correspondent showing her awesome energy over all with whom she had are to be had contact." - Mary Cowden Clarke, World-said girls: or, Types of womanly attributes of all lands and a while (1858)

"I attribute my achievement to this - I never gave or took any excuse." — Florence Nightingale

By the prevent of 1855, Nightingale grow to be some component of a cult determine, the epitome of all that have become appropriate and right in England. Indeed, she turn out to be visible through many, then and now, because of the reality the incredible accurate detail about the Crimean War, specifically due to the reality England took one critical beating after any other at a few stage within the struggle. Therefore, the authorities modified into simplest too satisfied to see the clicking offer Nightingale the attention, in preference to the listing of conflict disasters, and due to this adulation, the authorities authorized the advent of the Nightingale Fund on November 29, 1855. The cash it raised modified into now not for using the military but placed inside the palms of Nightingale herself to be used to set up a nursing faculty. A public meeting grow to be held to understand Nightingale and the fund. Sidney Herbert led the meeting and praised his famous buddy, saying, "I truly have in reality heard this kind of pretty account from a soldier, describing the comfort it modified into, even to peer Florence skip — 'She may additionally want to speak to one and to every different, and nod and smile to a many extra; — however she couldn't do it to all, ; we lay there with the aid of the use of masses; but we can also need to kiss her shadow because it fell, and lay our heads at the pillow over again, content material material cloth.' — What poetry there may be in these guys! I assume I recommended you of some other, who said, 'Before she came, there was such cussin and swearin; and after that, it became as holy as a church.'"

Nightingale herself become beaten with the useful resource of the usage of the triumphing, writing to Elizabeth Herbert on January 6, 1856, "In answer on your letter (which accompanied me to the Crimea and back to Scutari) presenting to me the mission of a Training School for Nurses, I will first beg to say that it's far not possible for me to explicit what I actually have felt in regard to the sympathy and the self perception tested to me with the resource of the originators and supporters of this scheme. Exposed as I am to be misinterpreted and misunderstood, in a subject of action wherein the work is new, complex, and far flung from many who take a seat in judgment upon it,— it is, surely, an abiding resource to have such sympathy and such appreciation introduced domestic to me inside the midst of labour and issues all but overpowering. I need to add, but, that my present paintings is which include I may want to by no means barren place for each different, as long as I see room to believe that what I may additionally additionally do right here is unfinished. May I, then, beg you to precise to the Committee that I accept their concept, furnished I may additionally additionally do so on their knowledge of this extraordinary uncertainty, as to at the same time as it is going to be viable to me to preserve it out."

Thanks to Nightingale's personal popularity, coins poured in from throughout the united states of the us and the Duke of Cambridge himself volunteered to chair the committee to determined the college. Thus, by the time she once more to England in early 1857, Nightingale had more than £30,000 available for her use. Writing at that factor, Clarke noted, "The object of the "Training School for Nurses," is to teach Nurses within the Central Institution, to practice them in the schools for such responsibilities which the severa high-quality hospitals already in existence present, and to deliver them out applicable for reinstruct one of a kind nurses, in branches of the determine enterprise; therefore putting in a kind of everyday university for nurses, that shall ramify at a few degree inside the whole the usa in its useful consequences. Thus, as a minimum, the prevailing idea of the group appears to be ; however its future info are judiciously left totally on the discretion of her who has proved herself consummately prepared to determine and act in this trouble ; and to whom, furthermore, the Fund is obtainable as a peoples' present of gratitude." Clarke went immediately to feature divine windfall to Nightingale's past sports activities and sought to curry need for her destiny paintings: "God direct and pace her in her new task, as he manifestly guided and protected her via the previous one! His blessing rests upon such unmarried-souled beings as Florence Nightingale; and it visibly re-emanates through the expanded advantages His grace permits her to shed upon mankind. Not most effective inside the direct advantages conferred by using this form of lady as Miss Nightingale, does her sacred rate stand determined out; but inside the oblique effects produced with the resource of her instance, is her heaven-despatched goodness provided to the arena. It is this idea — that she is an evidence of her Creator's vouchsafements to his creatures — that Miss Nightingale ought to put up to the gaze of admiring humanity. It ought to reconcile her to have her reasons canvassed, her individual scrutinized, her moves applauded; and moreover, at the equal time as her modest delicacy must reduce lower back from homage, allow her benignly don't forget that gratitude is an irrepressible feeling, and want to be yielded its eager and enthusiastic utterance. In Florence Nightingale all of the global glorifies a lady who embodies the principle of devotion, inside the widest feel of the phrase; real devoutness to God, — worshipping him by means of awesome service, in reaping advantages her fellow-mortals; and fervent consecration of herself to a high and immortal reason."

Unfortunately, the fame that delivered her the cash and the possibility to do even extra well furthermore made it hard to do the easy activity she felt referred to as to. Nightingale modified into constantly sought out to make a speech or take part in a few exclusive way, which includes a memorial event to honor the fallen, and she or he speedy determined out that she would have to show down most offers, the equal way a contemporary-day film big name can't constantly be available. For instance, in October 1856, a relative, Lydia Shore, appealed to her on behalf of the guys of Sheffield, who preferred Nightingale to put the cornerstone for a state-of-the-art memorial to the Crimea's fallen. She answered, "The reason stated to me for your letter has my personal sympathy. It may were most congenial with my emotions, on my go decrease returned from the dying-beds of such some of brave men to take a issue in it. I shall be with the men of Sheffield in spirit each time they execute their proposed plan. It is with actual ache that I experience forced to mention no the privilege which they offer to me, of laying the primary stone. But I agree with I shall extremely good honour the purpose of these courageous useless thru abstaining from acting to court docket docket that publicity which I bear in thoughts to have been my splendid impediment in the artwork I had been engaged in for his or her sakes ; impeding it by using the use of way of arousing in some minds contend with worldly differences. I will ask you to offer this letter to Mr. Overend; and I need to be satisfied that Mr. Overend should make identified to people who had expressed a choice that I need to lay the primary stone, my motives and my sorrow for now not doing so; and I ought to mention moreover that I enjoy an especial remorse in declining this at Sheffield, from old and steeply-priced circle of relatives reminiscences related with the vicinity. I must apologize for therefore late an answer, as I even have only virtually returned domestic."

After a outstanding deal planning and negotiation, Florence opened the Nightingale Training School at St. Thomas' Hospital on July 9, 1860. Her college students informed for 5 years earlier than going to artwork on the Liverpool Workhouse Infirmary in May 1865. At the time, no textbook had ever been written for those education to be nurses, so Nightingale wrote one, Notes on Nursing, in 1859, and it remained a fashionable textual content of the project for many years. It began, "Shall we start thru way of taking it as a present day precept — that every one Disease, at a few duration or other of its course, is more or masses less a reparative technique, not typically observed with suffering: an system, attempt of nature to treatment a way of poisoning or of decay, which has taken location weeks, months, on occasion years ahead, unnoticed, the termination of the disease being then, while the antecedent manner became happening, determined? If we take delivery of this as a stylish precept we're able to be proper now met with anecdotes and instances to show the opportunity. ... In looking ailment, every in private homes and in public hospitals the component which movements the professional observer most forcibly is that this, that the signs and symptoms and signs and symptoms or the sufferings normally considered to be inevitable and incident to the sickness are very often no longer signs and symptoms of the sickness in any respect, but of a few aspect pretty high-quality — of the want of glowing air, or of moderate, or of warmth, or of quiet, or of cleanliness, or of punctuality and care within the management of weight loss plan, of each or of all of those. And this quite as an entire lot in private as in sanatorium nursing." More than a century later, nursing expert Joan Quixley defined, "The e-book become the number one of its kind ever to be written. It appeared at a time even as the easy policies of health were only beginning to be recognized, on the same time as its topics were of critical significance...at the same time as hospitals were riddled with contamination, at the same time as nurses were nonetheless in particular seemed as ignorant, uneducated dad and mom. The ebook has, constantly, its vicinity inside the history of nursing, for it became written via the founding father of modern nursing".

Sadly, even as within the Crimea, Nightingale reputedly shrunk brucellosis, a virulent and habitual fever passed through unpasteurized milk and undercooked meat. She suffered for the rest of her lifestyles from frequent flare-united states of americaof the contamination, which brought on her yet again to pain notably and stored her bedridden an lousy lot of the time. However, she controlled to preserve her art work developing nursing applications, writing copious letters and receiving website online site visitors at her bedside.

With a excellent deal of her work focused on increasing the position of ladies in medication, Nightingale made the ambitious skip in 1859 of writing a letter of introduction to Sir Benjamin Brodie of the Royal College of Surgeons on behalf of Dr. Elizabeth Blackwell, the number one woman within the United States to graduate with a medical diploma. Though she and Blackwell need to have their versions over the years, on February 13, 1859, Nightingale wrote, "Do you don't forget me as having the advantage to be sufficiently acknowledged to you to ask you to do me a totally amazing kindness? The Bearer of this is an English woman, Miss Blackwell MD. Who graduated in America - has labored her way as tons as a physician's exercising amongst ladies and youngsters (no longer solely in midwifery) at New York, and is now once more to England wherein she can be very nerve-racking to have the advantage of your advocate as to her destiny profession, if you may spare her time for an interview."

Brodie

Portrait of Blackwell

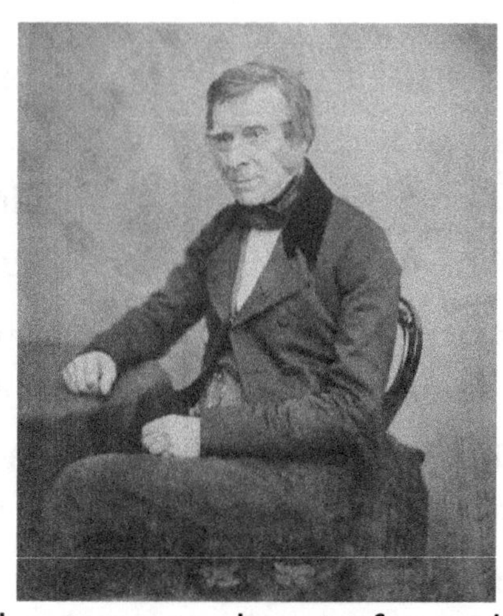

With the coronary heart of a real reformer, Nightingale modified into interested in every element related to the care of the sick and injured. In 1861, she went as a ways as to put up a layout of her very non-public for a brand new fashion of health center mattress, and she sent it to Civil Engineer Sir Robert Rawlinson, alongside component a charge estimate of £one hundred in keeping with mattress. This modified into a very excessive charge to pay and displays each her trouble for individuals who would possibly need to sleep inside the beds and a revel in of self belief in her investment. She admitted, "I want not thing out to you that a few adjustments should be made for a Civil Hospital - with ladies Patients. - that a better elevation may cheaply be procured by way of a piece extra treatment..."

By this time, Nightingale become considered an professional within the health and welfare of preventing guys. In 1862, she wrote a paper entitled "Army Sanitary Administration, and Its Reform Under the Late Lord Herbert", which become in flip take a look at in advance than the "Congres de Bienfaisance" in London in June. Toward the cease of the paper, she wrote, "Unsuccessful tries had been made to arrange a corps of orderlies, unconnected with regiments: the result become most unsatisfactory. Lord Herbert's committee proposed to symbolize a corps — the people of which, for regimental features, are to be carefully decided on through way of the commanding and scientific officers — specifically skilled for his or her obligations, after which related truely to the regimental medical institution, from which they can't be eliminated to the ranks, besides for proved disability or breach of location. This modified into carried into effect fast after his loss of life. Success of all The crowning testimony of the incredible national importance of the new the ones mea-system of sanitary management, inaugurated by using Lord Herbert, is...determined within the remaining Chinese day ride, wherein his reforms had been first Death fee nearly tested. An expeditionary pressure became despatched to the opportunity component of the sector, proper right into a adverse america, infamous for its epidemic illnesses. Every required association for the safety of fitness emerge as made, with the cease result that the mortality of this stress, which include wounded, come to be little more than 3 consistent with cent, consistent with annum, on the identical time because the 'constantly ill' in health center have been approximately just like at home. Let us assessment with this high-quality achievement what befell in the course of a former warfare in China. The twenty sixth Cameronians, a 'overall abstinence' regiment, and one of the fine and maximum wholesome in the British issuer, have emerge as landed at Chusan, 900 strong, and left to its fate without any sanitary care. In months only twenty guys is probably have been given collectively."

In addition to nursing, Nightingale also dedicated an entire lot of her efforts and interest to other tasks she taken into consideration important to human beings's health, even at the equal time as her personal fitness suffered. In March 1878, she wrote to a friend, "Overwhelmed with enterprise as I am, London has continuously been my home for the ultimate 21 years." She then delivered, "I am positive that you bid me God tempo in all my gadgets: the Training of Nurses which will become extra & greater critical each 12 months: the

Sanitary reform in our Army & america usually: the Sanitary development - & above all the "Irrigation improvement", to save you famines, of India: horrific heaps and thousands of our starving fellow topics."

The latter subject matter changed into a selected passion for Florence, who wrote a paper entitled "Life or loss of existence in India" for the National Association for the Promotion of Social Sciences assembly in Norwich in 1873. Part of it look at, "This exceptional crucial work of the law of the water of India is likely at this 2d the most essential query inside the worldwide; or instead not question — movement. Nothing can have a look at with it for the material progress of the people, and their moral development is notably established upon it: for, until the human beings are in a diploma relieved from their bondage to poverty and want, they cannot attend to different subjects. Another very important aspect, and in detail associated with irrigation in all methods, wishes to be taken up: and this is, the hassle of manufacturing in India. There are at this second as a minimum one hundred,000 horse water energy to be had and made little want of in the outstanding irrigation canals. The canals will bring the goods to and from manufactories, and the irrigation will let out heaps and hundreds from agricultural labour for such art work. With cheap labour, cheap strength, cheap carriage, and reasonably-priced meals, India may want to have the very maximum benefits for manufacture, for civilisation, and additionally for existence, and all that makes lifestyles well worth having to the ones whom God has created higher than the brutes, and extraordinary a bit 'decrease than the angels.'"

While Nightingale emerge as very inquisitive about relieving the suffering of these in the an extended way reaches of the empire, she also worked hard to keep the schooling she determined in the Crimea to undergo on poorest residents of every London and the rural regions. While she cherished a few achievement, she furthermore positioned out that antique conduct die difficult, especially a number of the undereducated. To triumph over this, she determined to be flexible and meet humans wherein they have been. In October 1895, she wrote to a Mrs. Leiter, regarding "Mrs. Cheadle's Short "Report" on our 'Health Missioners,'" younger ladies especially professional to care for and train new moms. "It came about to me as on your two suggestions 1. Of using the District Nurses…for Health Missioners and a couple of. That horrible women might likely no longer like instructions as to lyings-in & babies from younger single women. 1. That our professional District Nurses in London are preferred as "Health Missioners" and a couple of. That the horrific mothers have continuously welcomed their "Health" guidelines, that none are married, few are widows, & many are between 23 or 24 and

30. The horrible mothers revel in so snug after being attended to & washed via those Nurses that they will be glad to take care of their in addition recommendations."

One of the results of a long existence is being known as upon to help others whom one has recognised for a long time. In 1897, Nightingale wrote to Sir George Higginson on behalf of a nurse whom had gotten into some type of difficult situation. She started, "May I presume to write proper right down to you as Chairman of the "Home" Committee for the Gordon Boys Home to ask you to be so splendid as to investigate into the grounds of dismissal of Sister Constable from being Nurse to the sick boys. The look at given to her expires on Oct. 18." She then went at once to protect her pal, which incorporates, "If upon enquiry you discover that the charge made in opposition to her of being absent with out depart modified into both primarily based in reality upon a misconception on her issue or in any other case inadequate as the precept floor of dismissal, may additionally it no longer be feasible or equitable to supply her a few reimbursement after nine years' organization? As a Nurse professional in the "Nightingale Fund" School at St. Thomas' Hospital & afterwards as Nurse at the St. Marylebone Infirmary, I truely have said her well & have always taken into consideration her to be a strictly honest & honest woman & an exquisite Nurse. And that is my excuse for taking the freedom of creating this Suggestion."

Chapter 5: Early Life

Florence Nightingale have turn out to be the daughter of a privileged British couple, Frances Smith (1788-1880) and William Edward Nightingale (1794-1874). The Nightingales were wed in 1818 inside the Church of England through an evangelical clergyman, and could afterwards embark on a long honeymoon, wherein that that that they had their kids, Parthenope and Florence in 1819 and 1820, respectively. The two daughters have been named after the locales in which they have been born; Parthenope or "Pop" as she might moreover be identified, turned into named for a Greek settlement in which she have emerge as born in Naples. In Florence's case, she have turn out to be born within the famed Italian city, on the Villa Colombaia.

They in the end back to in England in 1821, developing a domestic of numerous circle of relatives houses in the following few years. In Derbyshire, they owned and managed a lead smelter. Afterwards, they moved to a extremely-modern domestic in Lea Hurst, in which they could stay till 1823 earlier than keeping it as a summer time domestic and moving to Kynsham Court in Herefordshire, then the Embley Park mansion in Hampshire in 1825. It modified into in Embley that Florence Nightingale could pay attention God's calling for company years later; she in fact become now not superb on the specifics of what that organisation entailed.

By severa debts, she had a primary epiphany and sense of calling in 1837, inspired by means of the usage of the works of Congregational minister, Jacob Abbott, at the same time as she have emerge as 16. She spent numerous months walking in the provider of disadvantaged human beings, uncertain of what purpose her calling added on, but moved with the useful resource of her religious feelings to behave. Some of the beneficiaries of her compulsion to serve had been the needy humans of the village close to her circle of relatives's domestic. Florence emerge as as involved in the lives of the lowest in society as she modified into in its pinnacle echelons; in 1839, she, her sister and cousins were even supplied to Queen Victoria.

Florence's letters from her early years might also display a sensitive, intellectually curious and introspective younger girl. She exchanged masses of correspondence with ladies who must inspire her to discover her faith – what is "unseen" – as a real and guiding strain within the gift, bodily, knowable international. According to a few university students, her religion seemed to be greater about spotting God's energy because it worked in live performance with the bodily global, in preference to some trouble that come to be completely divorced from it. It have grow to be view that reconciled the female's quality, medical mind alongside facet her enjoy of better reason.

Another key impact in her life have emerge as her Trinity College, Cambridge-knowledgeable father, William, who had began to train the ladies as early as 1825. He supported Florence and her sister's training, consequently she modified into decided in Latin and Greek, similarly to well-read in a number of genres. She delved into the have a take a look at of mystic saints like St. Teresa of Avila and St. John of the Cross. She studied the Italian poetry of Alfieri, Ariosto and Tasso. She studied European statistics. She must write complicated and eloquent analyses and manuscripts, in addition to do translations. She had a busy, fantastic mind, enriched with the resource of her father and different intellectuals she may additionally interact in letters and communique, amongst them, the biblical pupil, Baron Christian von Bunsen.

Florence's father William, but, changed into best supportive to some extent. In 1845, she preferred to research the nursing change from the nearby Salisbury Infirmary. But William, his spouse Fanny, and even Florence's sister Parthenope have been reportedly not pleased through Florence's choice to pursue the change — a vicinity of "menial paintings" that became now not considered appropriate for ladies of her lofty social fame on the time. She observed strategies round their disapproval; in 1846, her hobby became have become closer to government Blue Books, which had been reviews and references she relied upon, in the direction of coaching herself to become an professional on health facility problems of manage and sanitation. But it wouldn't be the first time one or of her family could get inside the manner of what grow to be perceived as an beside the point education for a nicely-introduced up extra younger girl. It has been said that during 1840, Florence's mom, Fanny, changed into even evidence towards Florence analyzing math — a subject that modified into now not visible as in particular relevant to nicely-born women on the time.

Chapter 6: Nursing before Nightingale

The phrase "nurse" is stated to derive from nutrice, a fifth Century Classical Latin time period for a moist nurse; a girl employed to provide breastmilk to an infant. This subsequently got here to mean a girl caregiver for youngsters, that is the manner it entered Middle English in the 13th century. The due to this increased over the following centuries, such that "nurse" have come to be someone being concerned for every other individual with the beneficial useful resource of the 15th century.

Legendary playwright William Shakespeare has an interesting location inside the records of nursing. His writings in Comedy of Errors (written within the late 16th century) holds one of the earliest documented uses of the English phrase, "nurse," in a very scientific context: "I will attend my husband, be his nurse, Diet his sicknesse, for it's far my Office..."

Nursing, however, has been round for a long way longer than The Bard and longer even than even the fifth century Latin nutrice wherein it lines its etymology. As prolonged as human beings have cared in myriad techniques for each different – for children, for the unwell, for the injured, for the elderly – there has usually been some semblance of nursing to be located in our statistics.

Buddhists and Ancient Greeks had a few element just like hospitals, as did the Roman Empire round three hundred A.D. The first traces of nursing as it's miles presently recognized is idea to had been within the latter, wherein a part of the empire's grand interests modified into to place something similar to navy hospitals anywhere they ruled, which in flip necessitated men and women tasked with the care of patients alongside aspect scientific doctors.

While it now appears to be in the maximum commonplace instinct to attend to the unwell, this was now not constantly the case in human records. In the Greco-Roman international, there has been a general disdain for vulnerable factor and illness. Hippocratic physicians had been standouts in vicinity of the guideline, within the feel that they took on an mindset of greater being concerned for his or her fellow human beings (the Hippocratic Oath, which has roots in the classical world, is still relevant nowadays).

The upward thrust of Christianity had masses to do with changing the an awful lot much much less charitable perceptions of humans of the time, which sooner or later had a heavy effect at the improvement of drugs. While generation and religion may often find out itself at odds, in the realm of early medication, the contributions of Christianity have been profitable. Jesus of Nazareth, who sits at the coronary coronary coronary heart of the Christian faith, had teachings like, "Whatever you did for one of the least of those brothers of mine, you likely did for me…" – a excellent distinction from cultures that placed a primacy on electricity and fulfillment at the price of being involved for "lesser" people.

When Greece embraced Christianity, for instance, many people grew to come to be far from lives of previous pricey toward the issuer of others. Women of privilege were particularly amazing for turning palaces into homes for the needy. Some also become patronesses to the religion and those who practiced and promoted it, within the sharing of their treasured resources. Some girls went even similarly than imparting assist and have emerge as deaconesses themselves. Tales have additionally been informed from the second century, of strategies patients of the plague can be tossed into the streets thru pagan households, at the same time as Christian organizations rallied round them.

The Byzantine generation, with its edicts on non secular tolerance, could only cultivate more of that present day revel in of charitable community welfare and social reform... due to the fact whilst Christianity have grow to be allowed to flourish, so became its humane technique to the "least" of society. Many houses, hostelries and hospitals ("Xenones") might be set up for the care of an array of goals like the ones of lepers, pregnant ladies and children. By A.D. 369, St. Basil of Caesarea might be founding the very first, massive sanatorium; it had 3 hundred beds and become organized like a present day medical institution, with numerous forms of wards and homes interior it for pretty a few precise functions. Christians may be related to the founding of hospitals on the same time as tons as our gift time.

In the Byzantine empire, many humans engaged in acts of nursing, such as high score ladies just like the Empresses, St.

Helen and later, Theodora. Most of them, however, were nuns and priests who took to nursing as although it have been prayer — a way of loving and serving their God. By the prevent of the 4th century, however, nursing duties may also be completed by using the use of using professionals who held immoderate repute in their groups. There were character men ("hypourgoi") and women ("hypourgisses"), and "nosokomoi" who were moreover like hospital directors, and "paranosokomoi," similar to assistants of nurses. There have been installed systems, guidelines to comply with and even punishments for transgressions (some faux moves merited excommunication for an afternoon!), and exhortations to deal with sufferers with careful hobby and kindness, and to technique their non secular art work with out fear.

Historical rulers who carried Christian standards and values might be bringing the same humane technique to the needy and its consequent medical effects to other components of the sector. Charlemagne, for instance, decreed that there be hospitals alongside cathedrals and monasteries in Western Europe in the early Middle Ages. In this and plenty of strategies, monasteries became essential to community life in Europe from the years 500-1100; that that that they had hospitals, provided schooling in recovery and as a result furthermore held libraries, herb gardens, and promoted particular exercises for supporting deal with the sick at the side of their prayers and other spiritual practices.

Several activities came about to create a decline in the have an impact on of the church on the scientific workout. Many monasteries had been in the rural areas and even as cities started out to rise, they have grow to be a whole lot less important to the existence of a community. Monks had been in the end disallowed from serving beyond their monasteries, which have been decided to be a large disturbance from their spiritual obligations. But sincerely because of the reality the non secular community couldn't provide beneficial beneficial aid did not mean the want have become no longer there; for this reason, the beginnings of lay human beings and the secular community being greater organized and concerned inside the exercising of drugs. Even then, even though, there have been a few illnesses that the non-spiritual feared to the touch and that the church still had to tackle a primary feature, as within the case of leprosy (the illness, no matter the whole thing, is a specially top notch one in the lifestyles and times of Jesus Christ).

Political changes have been each other detail in curbing the impact of the church at the development of drugs. During the reign of Henry VIII and the Reformation, monasteries got here beneath danger – and at the aspect of them, the welfare artwork that they did. Many of the needy were then left without aid, which ultimately brought on a non-spiritual-affiliated method to public health care.

The upward push of Christian hospitals wouldn't be as impactful once more till the religious revivals in Europe of the eighteenth century, with waves felt nicely past the continent; Christian pioneers are even credited for the founding of hospitals in "the New World." Medical missions are although being performed to numerous factors of the area, these days.

With the big role of organized faith within the traumatic of the ill, the reputation quo of hospitals and the training of caregivers, it is no wonder that many person contributors to Western remedy additionally have a few historical past inside the faith. Guy de Chauliac (1300–1368), celebrated health practitioner of the Middle Ages who in reality wrote the e-book on surgery that is probably used till the 17th century, emerge as a clergyman. Nicolaus Copernicus (1473 – 1543), famous for his art work in astronomy, modified right right into a priest and working toward doctor. Gregor Mendel (1822-1884), considered the founding father of modern genetics, became an Augustinian friar... and those are just a few examples. Innumerable exclusive religious individuals who did not always take legitimate vows might be amongst them - Florence Nightingale, covered.

The Calling of a Woman

With Christianity's ties to the clinical area, it's far in the end fitting then, that a lady of Florence Nightingale's religious ideals and convictions need to discover a calling inside the career of nursing. Unfortunately, her privileged circle of relatives did no longer precisely percentage her enthusiasm for the sector, and did not on the outset encourage her in its pursuit.

Where a few semblance of nursing modified into as soon because the province of awesome personalities just like the Empresses of Constantinople, or the "hypourgoi" and "nosokomoi" of excessive social repute, thru way of the Victorian generation in which Florence Nightingale lived, that come to be not pretty the case. There end up an order to "right" society which dictated gender and sophistication roles; not generally followed in the lower returned of closed doors, however at the least publicly codified and together aspired to.

Following the greater open indulgences of the Georgian era, the Victorians reverted to more pious aspirations, which covered the crafting of inflexible norms on gender roles and sensuality. It changed into truely George III who started the ball rolling with 1787's Proclamation For the Encouragement of Piety and Virtue, and for the Preventing and Punishing of Vice, Profaneness and

Immorality. His granddaughter, Queen Victoria's technology, have to in the end be most associated with putting higher bars and limitations on public morality – particularly sensuality - to earn an photo of prudery.

The precise impetus for change isn't regarded. Some historians say that shifts amongst debauchery and the recovery of values are cyclical; a product of massive society's preference for improvement, tremendous in many instances alongside global statistics together with the contemporary duration's shifts from liberal and modernist instructions to conservative and traditional. Some say that setting mores changed into the aristocracy's method of reasserting superiority and manage at the time, below threat from the Industrial Revolution's swelling center splendor. Others say the stern codes rose underneath Queen Victoria to restore the monarchy's picture, extended tarnished through manner of the use of her more extravagant predecessors. Either way, the rules were well-entrenched by the point Florence Nightingale heard her calling of issuer through nursing.

The profession turn out to be ugly to a circle of relatives of privilege for masses reasons. First among them become that it grow to be a career first of all – paid paintings changed into "declasse," or of a lower social repute. Women were furthermore anticipated to marry, raise kids and preserve a domestic, in desire to chasing after a profession. Every female, it have become encouraged, need to usually be a dutiful wife.

Nursing at the time, become consequently an nearly abhorrent opportunity for a girl of a excessive social repute. It end up paid work and ingesting of time and energy (in all likelihood far from domestic and circle of relatives). But even more than that, it become menial, strenuous, and in lots of strategies - like within the important handling of bodily fluids — considered degrading. Furthermore, it grow to be a interest that inextricably required anatomical information and bodily intimacy — but any other assignment to the gender norms of the time.

Consider, as an example, who changed into "stereotypical" of a nurse in advance than the iconic imagery of Nightingale's "The Lady with the Lamp" captured the overall public's creativeness - Charles Dickens' well-known fictional individual, Sarah Gamp, of The Life and Adventures of Martin Chuzzlewit (1844). She modified into an unprofessional, unpleasant determine of a woman, an incompetent nurse and a disreputable alcoholic.

A variety of things passed off to mission those perceptions. In no particular order:

Demographic Imbalances. Census research of the mid-1800s had been displaying a demographic fashion that regarded to signify the want for essential social exchange. English women have been outnumbering English guys thru the loads of lots. The implications of this end up profound. The concept espoused thru many on the time – that ladies were to be better halves, emerge as quantifiably not viable due to the fact there has been simply now not sufficient guys round to end up husbands. "Odd women" without a couple, therefore, had a problem... even as women from the top strata of society also can have households that could or would possibly "preserve" them, ladies from middle and reduce schooling needed to discover the manner with which to fund their very own futures.

Unfortunately, their options have been constrained because of the truth (1) paintings taken into consideration "suitable" for ladies come to be few; and (2) they had been no longer provided with educational possibilities to growth their present day employment alternatives. Thus, the demographic imbalance became one of the most crucial motives for education and employment for women within the 1850s. One of the most high-quality calls for addressing the issue changed into Harriet Martineau's 1859 article, "Female Industry." The piece, which regarded in the Edinburgh Review, changed proper right into a literature evaluate of writings on girls and the body of workers from the years 1843 to 1858. There have come to be reputedly an extended-taking walks, simmering need for changing girls's real home roles. There emerge as a want for them to have monetary independence thru wider education and employment.

The Rise of Nursing Sisterhoods. Acceptable professions for ladies at the time blanketed turning into governesses, instructors and paid partners. Eventually, this would moreover come to encompass the brand new-at-the-time, era of typewriting. Nursing as a substitute, on the same time as being ideal for girls, preferred a few extra adjustments to have an air of thriller of respectability.

Protestant nursing sisterhoods, which grew in variety in England at round this time, contributed to that. These sisterhoods crafted from extra privileged girls who paid to have a look at, whilst running-class women who did no longer need to pay, educated to paintings underneath the supervision of "Sisters." The sisterhoods ushered in systemic nursing training. The professionalism of nursing schools, along unpaid carrier furnished by the use of genteel Sisters, ascribed greater respectability for nursing thru the patina of philanthropy.

Nursing sisterhoods did no longer clearly enhance the photo of nursing as a profession. They additionally helped bring in extra girls into the body of workers. Unpaid members of sisterhoods were given room and board, however non-those who graduated from them determined outdoor employment. Higher rating, supervisory-degree nurses may furthermore skip right now to forge schooling schools and consequently, churn out even greater nurses who need to input the workforce. Earning girls from middle and top commands hence prolonged in amount.

"The Lady with the Lamp." Conditions rapid have become ripe for one more aspect to propel the sector of nursing to its rightful vicinity as a profession that demanded recognize and advocated aspiration. It changed into time for a photo, a rallying photo. An icon. Enter - Florence Nightingale.

Chapter 7: Travels and Education

Florence Nightingale had the method to tour significantly, and her destinations included various factors of Europe in conjunction with Rome and Greece. She had additionally toured Egypt. Her travels delivered her a few solace from her internal sorrows (greater on this in a communicate of private lifestyles, later); a Nightingale pupil had even described her suffering as specifically corresponding to or nearing a "intellectual breakdown." Travels additionally brought her to the direction of individuals who might encourage her to pay attention to 'God's voice' and assist her channel her calling to serve. In Rome, she met Roman Catholic nun, Laure de Ste. Columbe. In Athens, she met a missionary named Mary Stanley Baldwin. Her travels additionally introduced her the friendship of an American missionary named Mrs. Hill, and the acquaintance of Sidney Herbert, who may want to within the future name upon her understanding for a country extensive want and trade the course of her existence.

One of the most impactful travels she had ever undertaken have end up to Germany in 1850 and 1851. These gave her probabilities to check from the Kaiserswerth Deaconess Institution, a pioneering Protestant organisation for the development of Protestant deaconesses. It was based totally through the Lutheran minister, Theodor Fliedner years in advance, in October, 1836.

Pastor Fliedner become moved thru the works of Protestant Mennonites and Moravians, as well as the mind of Elizabeth Fry (a British, Quaker philanthropist pivotal to prison reform) in the direction of organizing women inside the helping of needy humans in society, together with orphans, the terrible and the unwell. In his institute, extra younger women may additionally take a look at the competencies crucial in the course of the accomplishment of that practical logo of religious carrier.

Florence changed into proper right right here as a probationer – a pupil – from July to October, 1851.

In 1853, she traveled to France and purchased similarly immersion into the life of nursing moved by the usage of manner of spirituality. She resided with nuns such as the Sisters of Charity, and worked with them in hospitals and orphanages. Travels together with those solidified the meaning of her call, immersed her in service, and knowledgeable her in organizational systems and systematized programs that would help actualize her aspirations of tending to the needy. They additionally confirmed her possible challenges she may additionally face.

Allowing for the hiring of women from all social instructions for example, especially those who may not exactly have the most moral backgrounds, might be met not handiest with resistance by manner of her pals, however via way of real demanding conditions to her utility. As she had seen, there can be consuming, awful behavior with male medical medical doctors and male patients, and social struggle maximum of the pupils from various backgrounds. Still, she persevered, compelled by using her calling to serve thru nursing. By a few payments, she even felt she had a calling to be a "savior-" which became complementary to her preference to nurse the needy in frame and in spirit.

As a lady of her time and unique higher elegance sports, however, pushed as she have become she however needed to bide her time and find out strategies of responding to her name on the identical time as appeasing her disapproving family. She determined possibility in The Establishment for Gentlewomen in the route of Temporary Illness.

Work Experience

In 1853, Florence Nightingale's father reportedly gave her a each year allowance of 500 kilos (approximately $40 to $50,000 in these days's cash). Support like this can permit her to make contributions of provider with fewer issues, and she or he did devote her time to well really worth causes.

The Establishment for Gentlewomen at some point of Temporary Illness have turn out to be based totally thru Lady Charlotte Canning and a cadre of various female philanthropists in 1849, and opened its doors in 1850. Its aim end up to provide nursing care to women of modest approach suffering temporary infection. These had been knowledgeable ladies who fell the various high social strata that would control to pay for private care, and the least of society who won admission to public hospitals. The Establishment changed proper into a modest one itself, with a handful of beds and circle of relatives employees, plus nurses while wanted and physicians and surgeons contributing their facts free of charge.

It did no longer pretty flourish in its early years, plagued via problems in staffing key positions like that of the residence Matron, and of finding ideal nurses. The Ladies Committee decided salvation in attractive Florence Nightingale because the residence's Lady Superintendent. Nightingale agreed but introduced conditions of her non-public; that she be accorded the freedom to reorganize the Establishment as she noticed fit; and that she be allowed to utilize it as a shape of nursing university. She were given her wish, and the Committee have been given their Lady Superintendent in 1853. The active reformer started working promptly, and comprehensively.

Around this time, centers had been advanced, such that there was heat water supply on all flooring and a simple machine emerge as established to deliver up warm food immediately from the kitchens within the basement. She prepared for better providers for coal and groceries. She furthermore instituted changes in admission requirements for girls looking brief care. The facility became non-denominational, and opened its doorways to ladies associated with clergy and the protection force (preceding to that, they'd catered in maximum instances to sick governesses). There had been mild charges for a space, however rate moreover needed to come alongside letters of introduction; a assure of fee of charges; and a scientific certificates attesting to the girls's situations, as a few ailments, including highbrow and infectious, did now not fall inside the purview of the organization. She had been given busy speedy, but her time with the agency may be quick, and he or she wouldn't have the possibility to realise her motive of setting up a nursing college via her art work right right right here.

The Ladies Committee had engaged Nightingale's records simplest in 1853. She did different artwork within the early 1850s, which consist of volunteering at a clinic in Middlesex at some point of a cholera outbreak. But through 1854, she might be far from London and making even extra impactful changes in a bigger global. Britain had joined the Crimean War, and her soldiers had been loss of life. They desired a savior of a particular brand of talents and spirit.

They desired a person like Florence Nightingale.

"The Lady with the Lamp"

The Crimean War (1853 – 1856) turn out to be stimulated with the resource of manner of some of complex elements, amongst them, an expansionist Russia wielding the banner of Christian safety and threatening Turkey on the only hand; and Britain, France, Sardinia and the Ottoman Turks with a miscellany of hobbies on the possibility. The Brits had been mainly involved with how Russian aggression in Turkey need to have an impact on their commercial pastimes and strategic positions in India and the Middle East.

The Crimean War is considered thru many historians as 'the number one current struggle.' A lot of its tendencies can be decided within the wars of extra modern-day-day times, and some of upgrades alongside its period had been used inside the wars to have a look at it. The Crimean War worried vital international powers in alliance with every one-of-a-kind. It have become the first to have long-variety communications among leaders at home and troops in foreign theaters of warfare via telegraph. There have been mass-produced weapons and lengthy-range cannons from naval attack ships. Sea mines were used. There were innovations in steel, in industrially produced and greater accurate rifles, in armored warship technology. Railways made huge impacts in crafting inexperienced supply routes. There have been even enhancements inside the kitchen; society chef, Alexis Soyer, an energetic reformer himself, advanced the food regimen of troops with the invention of the Soyer Stove, a device that would be utilized by the British army for the following century. There have been also upgrades in fashion – the Balaclava helmet (basically a ski mask), the Raglan sleeve or maybe the Cardigan have been legacies of the Crimean War, and a testament to the hard conditions faced with the aid of troops and what they had to stay warmth and in form to fight.

The Crimean War modified into also the number one to be closely included with the resource of the media – struggle correspondents ought to get records domestic through telegram in as little as a few days. It have become the primary war to apply warfare pics. Letters despatched home through infantrymen seemed in newspapers too.

The wonderful degree of records available to the general public created a clamor for boosting the state of affairs of the troops being sent distant places once the gravity of their plight – that they've been laid low with injuries but even extra from forget - have end up stated. There become a dearth of materials and illness changed into rampant. Proper scientific attention have become unavailable, and the hospitals catering to the wounded and sick had been crushed and understaffed. 25,000 British lives could be out of place over the direction of the war (the be counted quantity wide variety for French troops can be higher at one hundred,000 and for Russians, over one million).

Wartime Nurse

In October 1854, then Secretary of State, Sidney Herbert, whose acquaintance

Florence Nightingale made in her travels, wrote to her seeking out help for the soldiers' state of affairs within the Crimea. She may have organizational control, however the price might be to the government. Reportedly internal days, she become capable of accumulate a band of nurses to go together with her to Scutari, Balaclava in Turkey (in which there has been a British health center base installation at some stage inside the warfare), on a challenge to offer comfort to the ill soldiers. This batch of nurses, approximately 3 dozen, blanketed gentlewomen and women from "lesser" backgrounds. There had been Roman Catholic Sisters; Anglican Sisters; and nurses from certainly one of a kind houses and hospitals throughout the usa of a. The institution left for the warzone underneath the control of Florence Nightingale, who secured their services thru contracts and geared up them with what might ultimately be iconic nursing uniforms.

The uniforms were each an equalizer and identifier for the nursing corps. While in uniform, all of the ladies had been truely nurses (alternatively of having splendor variations), entitled to the same meals and the equal resorts (the ones inside the non secular orders have been allowed to put on their behavior, but). The uniform changed into significantly regarded as horribly unflattering - set in plenty of dull grays, produced from a dress, a jacket, a white cap, a cloak and a headband figuring out the wearer as on foot on the Scutari Hospital. The uniforms have been unattractive sufficient, however this modified into in addition exacerbated via way of the rate by manner of the usage of which they have been wanted via the nurses, such that right sizing and tailoring changed into not even with. They have been made in primary sizes and handed out as fast as they were wished and available. But they surely identified — and greater importantly, included — the nurses. In a camp like Scutari, which had prostitutes and drunks, squaddies knew to hold their arms off of "Miss Nightingale's" girls.

Previous education and experience, uniforms and contracts couldn't have prepared absolutely everyone for what the nurses determined upon achieving the barracks health center. The scenario in Scutari grow to be nothing quick of scary. The medical institution modified into basically on a cesspool. Water modified into badly inflamed or in such brief supply that it turn out to be rationed. Patients languished in their very very own waste on a large amount of disorganized stretchers. There modified into a scarcity of materials, even the most fundamental requirements – cleansing cleaning cleaning soap and bandages. There had been rodents and bugs and distinct vermin. Soldiers were falling unwell with preventable ailments along with cholera and typhoid. No surprise the hospitals had a horrible popularity; it has even been said that a soldier have become seven times more likely to perish upon admission than on the fields of battle.

They now not handiest needed to warfare in opposition to the difficulties of the activity available; similarly they needed to fight resistance from male army medical doctors and workforce who were on site, who felt that the involvement of the women emerge as a mild on their abilities and professionalism. Need received over resistance but, and soon, the girls commenced strolling. They drafted a number of the in a position patients into provider, too. The hospital have end up wiped clean out, scrubbed from top to backside. Under Florence Nightingale's control, meals advanced for patients too, with an "invalid's kitchen" serving more wholesome fare. Clean linens were available from advanced laundry structures and from the ladies contributing to the showering themselves. The ladies had even belief of the soldiers' goals for enjoyment and highbrow pursuits; they positioned up a library and wrote letters home on behalf of squaddies.

Most memorably, Florence confirmed the maximum devotion and compassion to the unwell soldiers as "The Lady with the Lamp" – at night time time, she made diligent rounds a number of the rows of stretchers. This iconic regular ultimately earned her some special identify, "Angel of the Crimea."

By a few estimates, the presence of Florence Nightingale and her corps of nurses decreased the death price of squaddies on the health facility through way of -thirds.

Fame, Facts and Fiction

Or did they?

Scholars need to take a look at that now not the whole thing said about Florence Nightingale have come to be real, probably now not even the subjects she became maximum famous for. Improving sanitation on the fight hospital and the following development in mortality charges, for example, changed into probable because of a visit from the British authorities's sanitation commission in area of Florence Nightingale. Some debts even move to this point as to undertaking now not top notch overinflated attributions of her contributions to the welfare of soldiers in a few unspecified time within the future of the battle, however to mention that she would probably have even been damaging to them. A debatable film with the aid of the BBC, for example, might be contested through the use of nursing teachers for an destructive depiction of the heroine, showing lack of life rates on the medical institution below Florence's rate, as higher than the prices in a single-of-a-type regimental hospitals. Her defenders have to say depictions like these are deceptive; the in the end lethal, unsanitary situations she needed to cope with have been beyond Nightingale's manipulate because of the reality the hospital stood upon a defective sewer. Furthermore, they contended that some of the deceptive assaults were never supplied in peer-reviewed books or journals that might have opened them to a greater important and inflexible eye.

Some critics moreover say that the awesome deeds related to Nightingale's name have been ones that had been exaggerated and that she herself in no manner claimed to within the first location. She grow to be lionized as a nurse, as an example, but her actual, palms-on nursing experience end up very restrained and he or she or he emerge as certainly presupposed to be extra of an administrator and later in existence, a nursing theoretician.

Nevertheless what is understood to be actual is by using the use of many debts, heroic enough. Florence Nightingale changed into genuinely within the medical institution in Scutari and her information in the end contributed to the improvement of the lives of squaddies; folks that suffered there, and soldiers who can also need to inside the destiny comply with them in destiny fields of combat.

Aside from her nursing / administrative contributions, she end up moreover a mathematician; the primary female in the Royal Statistical Society, as a rely of reality, and now not truely a person who had passing knowledge of it. Her level of information of the hassle allowed her to make statistical analyses on death charges at some level within the war and factors that would have inspired it, which allowed her to complete a relationship amongst cleanliness and sanitation with survival results, and intelligently debate and lobby for them.

After the Crimean War, she reportedly located that of the British deaths, 16,000 had been brought on not via war accidents, but from problems like sickness, that can had been avoided with higher hygiene, sewage disposal and better desired medical institution control. When she came domestic, armed at the side of her firsthand information, "road cred," and the heartbreaking numbers, she lobbied politicians for health reforms for the warzone and for civilian hospitals. And they knew to be aware about the passionate reformer.

At the time, few names carried as a whole lot cachet as that of "The Lady with the Lamp." The find out have turn out to be one she can also deliver for the relaxation of her existence and well beyond it. The poet Henry Wadsworth Longfellow helped to immortalize the photo via his artwork, Santa Filomena, which included the traces: "A Lady with a lamp shall stand. In the exceptional facts of the land, a noble form of true, Heroic Womanhood..."

In this and loads of techniques, Florence Nightingale have emerge as a reluctant movie star. She spent a yr and a half in the warzone, and reportedly again domestic first-rate as soon as the conflict got here to a resolution in 1856 while the Russians were overwhelmed and in the end sued for peace. She changed into met with the beneficial resource of an surprising hero's welcome. It wasn't the best way her domestic america could have fun her achievements; Queen Victoria end up earlier of the sport even as she furnished Nightingale with a brooch, the "Nightingale Jewel" the twelve months earlier, in recognition of her proper paintings. The monarch and Prince Albert may want to moreover get maintain of her upon her move back to talk about her research and viable factors of reform. The government is likewise said to have talented her with $250,000 for her achievements. But Florence could moreover be commemorated because of the reality the trouble of many songs, poems and plays. She declined receptions and one-of-a-kind public honors, however received masses of letters thanking her for her carrier.

In 1856 she was a hero and a paragon of the tremendous Victorian. She modified right into a image of morality, hard artwork, employer and braveness. She had humility and modesty. She was a patriot. She end up nicely-bred and a woman caregiver and nurturer, however moreover had mind and grit. She had the respect and gratitude of many men for her deeds, and the admiration of girls for the instance she set and the boundaries she driven thru for them to analyze and locate decent, beautiful artwork.

But she have come to be also only in her mid-30s of age. Florence Nightingale modified into a long way from executed and he or she or he now had the voice to make more modifications.

In 1858, her work, Notes on Matters Affecting the Health, Efficiency and Hospital Administration of the British Army. Founded Chiefly at the Experience of the Late War. Presented through Request to the Secretary of State for War., emerge as published. It distinct her observations on the Crimean War, an assessment of what she had visible and professional, and pointers for reform.

She had a present for speaking her understanding, and is even identified for being an early person of pie charts (even though she did now not invent them) in her works. Her written output turned into amazing; she modified right right into a tireless creator of letters, books, evaluations and pamphlets. What is particularly interesting is that she modified into barely compensated for them; in line with one Nightingale scholar, she turned into paid (reportedly a pittance) for really one e-book, Notes on Nursing: What it is, and What it is not (1860) – the rest were written without pay, or found out together together along with her private cash both for personal use or for understanding sharing. One piece of writing she had even declined credit score score for; she penned The Institution of Kaiserswerth at the Rhine for the Practical Training of Deaconesses in 1851 upon the request of its visionary founder, Pastor Theodor Fliedner. Her gifted mind, shared so generously, may have an great impact on human health care. Some of her well-known writing paintings at the mission encompass:

- Subsidiary Notes as to the Introduction of Female Nursing into Military Hospitals in Peace and War, Presented with the resource of Request to the Secretary of State for War (1858)

- A Contribution to the Sanitary History of the British Army During the Late War with Russia (1859)

- Notes on Hospitals (1859)

- Notes on Nursing: What it's miles, and What it isn't always. (1860)

- Army Sanitary Administration and its Reform beneath the Late Lord Herbert (1862)

- Observations on the Evidence Contained within the Stational Reports Submitted to the Royal Commission at the Sanitary State of the Army in India (1863)

- Introductory Notes on Lying-in Institutions. Together with a Proposal for Organizing an Institution for Training Midwives and Midwifery Nurses. (1871)

- On Trained Nurses for the Sick Poor (1876)

The writings listed above do now not however even embody reflections on faith and her calling, or letters she had exchanged to her many friends and mentors, or addresses she made on her hassle of facts. She had even written insightful notes on her Bible.

She had a hectic mind and a coronary coronary heart for motion. Aside from being a prolific creator, in 1860, it modified into said that she used her authorities prize to help determined The Nightingale Training School for Nurses in London, at St. Thomas' Hospital. Through her example and people schools, she advised the nursing profession an extended manner a protracted way from the cool animated movie Charles Dickens had popularized in Sarah Gamp, via difficult education regimes that extended knowledge and skills in organized curriculums and scientific schooling, at the side of a advertising and marketing and marketing of strict codes of behavior. Women from all social instructions enrolled to teach in her hassle. She had stepped forward nursing into an honorable career any girl, even the ones in wealthy society, have to aspire to.

The Crimean War had helped Florence Nightingale find her calling and her voice. But it would moreover gift her with health traumatic situations for the relaxation of her life. During her time in Scutari, she stuck Crimean fever in 1855; it modified into stated to be a bacterial infection that would in no way genuinely go away her. She modified into an achieved female at the age of 36 while she lower decrease back to England, however by the time she modified into 38, she have end up regularly bedridden and mainly homebound. Contemporary historians and college college students of her existence even placed forth the idea that she suffered from Post-Traumatic Stress Disorder ("PTSD"), which might not were diagnosed to the Victorians at the same time as she emerge as alive.

The conditions and reviews of her nursing art work in the Crimea have been anyways, traumatic with the aid of using manner of maximum payments - 20-hour workdays, simply miles of beds about 20-inches apart, filled with the beneficial useful resource of a regular movement of injured and ill soldiers... In her first iciness in Scutari, three,000 of those guys died no matter her difficult work. Some of the signs and signs and symptoms of PTSD regarded to be observable in her latter behavior too; she had remoted herself upon her pass back, reportedly in no manner referred to her wartime studies or make public appearances or attend public capabilities, nor did she ever right now minister to the unwell yet again, as even though in avoidance of activities paying homage to her studies in the Crimea.

We will probably in no manner recognize if she suffered for this reason, but what is at the least clean is that in spite of her greater fitness stressful conditions, her zeal to make contributions did now not wane. She controlled to reply to that now not possible to face up to name to serve, even from the confines of home.

From her residence in Mayfair, she entertained appointments from politicians and one of a kind visitors who wanted her inputs. She pushed her health care advocacies, but became additionally frequently looked for her statistics. She consulted with a miscellany of events on numerous problems, amongst them, the going for walks of field hospitals throughout the usa' Civil War. She became moreover consulted on subjects of public sanitation in India.

Other honors she may be showered with are the Order of Merit, conferred to her by way of King Edward in 1907; and King George himself despatched her a birthday message whilst she have become ninety years vintage in 1910. It is an particularly nicely-deserved honor that International Nurses Day is widely diagnosed yearly at the day of her starting, the 12th of May.

Chapter 8: The Private Florence Nightingale

A lady is a complex creature with many faces, and superb though she can also had been, Florence Nightingale have come to be like many women on this experience.

We, a public from greater than a century after her existence, apprehend her from a mixture of facts and fiction. We see her vital achievements, we stay prosperously because of her contributions, but we do now not usually apprehend the internal adventure that drove her to such exceptional acts. Furthermore, now not all of the feats attributed to her are deserved, and not all of the facts approximately her are well known.

She also can have seemed informed and positive, however she harbored quite some hesitations and tension too, and had written out determined prayers virtually as she had written out authoritative works on her nursing and fitness care expertise. She struggled collectively together with her way ahead each from without — closer to the need of her family and the conventions of her society — and from inner — in struggling together along with her very very own weaknesses and temptations. She have become a woman beneficiant of her time and skills, a lady moved thru ethical imperatives to do what changed into wanted and what became proper, however she had flaws, weaknesses and biases too. She had such deep and personal sorrows — "There isn't always any a part of my life," she had as quickly as written, "upon which I can look decrease decrease back without pain."

She come to be in brief, human. With human concerns and human entanglements and human feelings.

Anguish in Privilege

The Nightingales were an wealthy circle of relatives and Florence grew up in elite social circles. They have been of this form of recognition that they have been deemed worth of being furnished to the Queen. As a further barometer of the shape of lifestyles that they had, do not forget that their own family domestic in Hampshire had no much less than 70 gardeners, and that Florence Nightingale wouldn't understand a way to do her own hair till she come to be over 30 years antique.

As may be seen in Florence Nightingale's biography, her privilege is that which underlies all of the opportunities she had for education, excursion, immersion, and influential networks that might sooner or later come collectively to help her gain her lofty dreams. But that isn't always to mention that she had an clean life.

She emerge as a sickly baby, the weather in England in no way pretty suiting her similarly to the best inside the Italian town of Florence in which she have become born. She determined connecting with special youngsters difficult, announcing in her illuminating, brutally honest Curriculum Vitae of 1851 that she did not quite discover herself to recognize "the performs of various children." She had prone wrists and wouldn't discover ways to write until the age of eleven or 12 (but oh how she might make up for it!), and modified into brought up by way of a governess vulnerable to severity (regardless of the fact that Nightingale did generously describe her as "properly intentioned").

From the age of 10, which become while her father William had involved himself in the intense and whole schooling of his daughters, Florence had an insatiable starvation for know-how such that for years, she "notion of little else but" however enriching her mind. She had a profound love of tune too, however a ordinary sore throat ought to prevent its critical pursuit. She observed the blessing of God even on this deprivation of some component that captured and inspired quite a few her passion and imagination no matter the truth that, as it freed her to pursue what she in the long run perceived as her actual calling – nursing.

She determined God's hand in her life right right here and in masses of excellent techniques, writing in addition in her Curriculum Vitae that "God has typically led me of Himself." Thus, as a sickly little one with a excessive governess, who entertained desires of hospitals and worrying for the ill, considered it as markers of the route God became calling upon her to serve.

But in advance than she might also need to take concrete steps in that route, she needed to take multiple detours. She modified into defined as awkward in social settings, alternatively averse to public hobby, and changed into in a complicated courting together together with her mom and sister, who appeared to were not capable of understand her — ultimately, it might were tough for max humans to recognize why a woman of wealth, immoderate social reputation and each worldly consolation may need the life of a nurse, with its inextricable menial tough artwork and its then unlucky affiliation with deplorable figures. Later in existence, she might also concede that she understood why her mother can be so frightened of her pursuit of the sector. But within the intervening time, she have become saved from her fervent desires, now not that she herself honestly understood her calling at the same time as she modified into younger; it'd ache her too, as visible in her jotted mind and complicated deliberations.

Her presentation at court docket docket heralded the begin of her society life, and there she became showed tempting, worldly glories. She defined eloquently her problems of the time, years earlier than she have emerge as a dwelling legend after the

Crimean War – "I wandered approximately within the Desert… on the lookout for bread and finding none. Then I took stones and consume them… because of the fact I have become starved." In the absence of non secular pride, she for a time, relished something satisfaction she need to locate of that excessive society life that end up so effects inner her draw close.

She struggled with reconciling what she felt changed into her calling from God with the opportunities and expectations of her family and her social fame. She had to triumph over their disapproval of her goals, in addition to the perceptions of huge society. She come to be, as an instance, predicted to marry properly and function youngsters; she in no way did, although not for loss of to be had offers. Over her lifetime, she needed to location a marriage idea or . In the technology wherein she lived, marriage should have almost genuinely relegated her duties to the residence component, while she had an entire lot one-of-a-kind pastimes for herself. Marriage have to have additionally nearly truly saved her within the social sphere she positioned so little delight in; "and fine such a wedding may additionally want to I without a doubt have."

In 1844, she declined a proposal of marriage from a cousin, Henry Nicholson. Henry have been on the circle of relatives home of Lea Hurst to teach her math whilst she come to be a more youthful female. When she refused his provide, it have turn out to be stated that the individuals of the circle of relatives among their households have turn out to be strained, with the Nicholsons shunning the Nightingales for a while afterwards. It changed into no less complex in the Nightingale own family; the refusal become reportedly a thing of contention among Florence on one facet, and her mom and sister at the alternative.

In 1849, she ought to say no to each distinct idea. Richard Monckton Milnes – gentleman, baby-kisser, English poet, customer to writers and subsequently the primary Baron Houghton of Great Houghton – could have been seemed as more than a suitable in form. Furthermore, she positioned him intellectually stimulating and became romantically interested in him too. He reportedly made his suit for years, however she would turn it down because of her moral compulsion to behave on her calling in the direction of nursing agency, and to percent her talents past the house existence. Some biographers word that her refusal of Milnes' concept may not were unequivocal; it modified into possibly extra of a "perhaps" than a "no." But whether or not or not or no longer there's some truth to that, as we recognize now, their romance by no means have emerge as a few difficulty greater than that. She did, however, manage to preserve a friendship with each men. Henry's wartime letters have been reportedly a supply of statistics for Florence, and Milnes supported her later reasons.

Marriage gives apart, exceptional instances had Florence struggling to apprehend and fulfill her calling. She made small, repeated attempts to be in the company of others. She tried schooling at a village school, but her health failed and her mom tried to prevent her from continuing on – she permit herself be avoided, feeling that she became both way no longer doing a great system due to the fact her education did now not make her licensed. She visited with the village horrific too, but she determined such efforts dissatisfying. She decided distaste in preaching them persistence even as she changed into so snug in life. She contemplated that to visit with the bad in her carriage, handing out cash modified into not Christ-like in any respect, for Christ "...made Himself like his brethren."

At any charge, the own family's active social life come to be taking up a number of her time. For 3 months of the 12 months they were in London for the season. Six months had been spent inside the u . S . At Hampshire, in which a dispersed village life modified into not conducive to her efforts. Three months of the only year end up spent overseas domestic in Derbyshire, in which they had been constantly appropriate and he or she modified into anticipated to be to be had to traffic similarly to sociable. She visited with villages anyplace and every time she may want to, however the ones sports have been not enough to satisfy her call.

Throughout her distractions, she felt that God and her calling in no way pretty left her on my own. She had written that every time she modified into untrue to her vocation, she suffered. But as her existence unfold out, slowly she have become brought about the existence that might absolutely improve her hungry soul. A chain of sports led one into every other, and peppered with unexpected advantages like her overly worried mom in some way allowing her to move on her immersive travels, she became capable of actualize what she felt her God wanted her to perform in lifestyles.

By 1851, she became a probationer – a pupil – at the Institute of Kaiserswerth, reflecting on the road that led her there in her insightful Curriculum Vitae (from which the charges on this phase have been sourced). Her time at Kaiserswerth need to ultimately be observed thru possibilities at The Establishment for Gentlewomen all through Temporary Illness in London in 1853, and in 1854, her legend-making year-and-a-half of at Scutari ultimately of the Crimean War. She felt her God come to be guidance her closer to her remaining calling even as she wrote Curriculum Vitae in 1851, and likely she changed into proper.

Even after her achievements and consequent fame within the Crimea, but, she reportedly had one more marriage offer to refuse - that of Sir Harry Verney, a flesh presser, who could in all likelihood later marry Florence's sister, Parthenope, alternatively.

Chapter 9: Later Struggles

After her bypass again from the Crimea, the bulk of her struggles reputedly associated with her health. As modified into earlier discussed, she also can have been plagued through way of the persistent and normal results of the Crimean fever she had shrunk whilst in Scutari in 1855. She can also additionally furthermore have additionally been by way of manner of PTSD. There is an unfortunate popular concept that she suffered from syphilis, however there can be no evidence of this. Some historians may recommend rather that she can also have suffered from Crimean fever, PTSD and an undiagnosed bipolar infection, or possibly a degenerative mind ailment like Alzheimer's.

Either way, her fitness difficulties increased over time. In 1861, she have grow to be gravely unwell and now not in a position to stroll, desiring assist with mobility for the subsequent years. By 1867, she have emerge as locating problems with interest.

One with the aid of one she out of place her circle of relatives – her father in 1874, her mom in 1880, and her sister in 1890, but before that, she grow to be pressured with supporting to manipulate their care. By 1896, she might be bed room-positive, this time for the rest of her lifestyles. Just some years afterwards, in 1902, he misplaced the prepared functionality to study and write and thru February, 1910, she changed into not capable to speak. She need to die a few months later, at the thirteenth of August, 1910.

In maintaining collectively collectively together with her personal nature, her own family reportedly declined a country extensive funeral and a Westminster Abbey burial, and her memorial upon a own family tombstone is marked, definitely, "F.N. Born 1820. Died 1910." She have become 90 years vintage.

A Surprisingly Complicated Legacy

Florence Nightingale's voice grow to be recorded in 1890, and of the precious few lines she had spoken have been the terms, "When I am not even a memory, handiest a name…"

A century after her loss of life, she wouldn't be wrong. She is a name well-known, but folks that had identified her and feature firsthand reminiscences of her are thru now all misplaced too, not that each person surely could possibly have acknowledged the depths of this form of complex girl. Even with all the mind she had located pen and paper to, despite the fact that she had a well-documented lifestyles from having been in the limelight for the nearly 60 years a few of the time she rose to fame and the time of her lack of existence, she nonetheless remains a thriller.

Her photo shows her as a nurse, but of her ninety years of existence, barely 3 may find her as one.

Her writings show her pressure in the direction of the fulfillment of what she believed turned into the selection of God. But to one of a kind human beings, she grow to be extra intellectual, bold, ego-driven and/or manipulative than genuinely compassionate. Her sister, Parthenope, for example, had as soon as written a pal that Florence modified into probably greater interested in the highbrow a part of nursing work than charity. A few exclusive letters need to emerge from the time she come to be alive, through the humans she had been in contact with, and people might be of a similar, now not-pretty-so-saintly vein. Sir John Hall, who grow to be in the Medical Services in 1854-fifty six, allegedly known as her formidable and seeking out energy. Then all over again, it is able to were a protective reaction from a member of the male hooked up order being challenged with the useful resource of a decided interloper of a woman, or a person feeling vexed via what he perceived as her unsubstantiated lionization.

People credit her for professionalizing nursing, but a few pundits contend that Nightingale's view was certainly the opportunity. To her, nursing became a vocation in preference to a career and that if her imaginative and prescient came into fruition, nursing have to as a substitute resemble the values and structures of a nunnery. She had even contested a proposed machine of professional nursing registration – but, this will be both because she favored to preserve it as a vocation, or she disapproved of the contents and approach of registration.

Florence Nightingale additionally, inextricably, have become a feminist icon – besides, her later writings ought to expose perspectives counter to feminism as we currently conceive of it (she seemed to simply accept as proper with specifically roles for which ladies need to excel and reportedly positioned many ladies unsympathetic and unqualified), and she or he became moreover defined as extremely of a reluctant and overdue champion for one of the key feminist issues of her time, that of women's proper to vote. Still, her views do now not cut price her from being a picture and example of braveness, will, expertise and achievement.

And so we're although left with such loads of questions. What was she in fact, saint or sinner? An egoist or the paragon of modest service? Was she a feminist or a sexist misogynist? Is it even proper to don't forget her a nurse in its everyday enjoy? But some facts do stay.

In phrases of practical effect, probably her motivations, non-public life and personal perspectives can take a backseat to the immoderate great modifications that her existence's art work and photo had ushered – whether they may be because it must be credited or not, whether or now not they have been by means of manner of the usage of planned layout or no longer, whether or not they had been encouraged via way of using altruism or ego, whether or not or now not or no longer she have become a feminist or now not. She promoted compassion. Helped beautify health center management and sanitation. Ushered extra instructional and employment possibilities for girls. Raised a country's spirits at a time of struggle. Inspired feminists. She is even inspiring some contributors the LGBTQ community, some of whom consider she may were a lesbian due to her refusal of conventions of marriage and rumored enchantment or even love for distinct girls. She inspired nursing colleges and programs and reportedly, Red Cross founder, Henri Dunant.

Whatever we're all driven by way of way of, sometimes the narratives of our lives escape our very private intents and designs. In the case of Florence Nightingale, inside the very last stability, it seems very masses that her existence become one which she had used, and that has been utilized by others, to make high-quality contributions to the world.

changed into every the happiest and the unhappiest day that seven-three hundred and sixty five days-antique Florence Nightingale had ever spent at Tapton in Yorkshire, England. The day began out in her grandmother's fine house with a breakfast so extremely good that Florence misplaced her everyday reticence.

"There are extra desserts and fruit than I even have ever seen in my life!" she gushed.

"An accomplishment really," agreed one of the many adults furthermore at breakfast, "for the reason that English breakfast is quite the superb in the international except."

"Flo will speedy have a double-uncle and a double-aunt," quipped each other, the usage of Florence's shortened name. Almost honestly all of us abridged Florence's call to 'Flo'. Her sister's call Parthenope modified into reduced to the two-syllable 'Parthe', simply so it rhymed with Marthy. But now and again Flo chopped Parthenope all of the manner proper all of the way down to 'Pop'!

The wedding ceremony which have grow to be to take place that afternoon in Tapton come to be uncommon. The bride have turn out to be the sister of Flo's father William. The groom became the brother of Flo's mom Fanny. So Flo could clearly have Aunt Mai an aunt twice over and Uncle Sam an uncleinstances over. And all in their future kids could be Flo's 'double-cousins'.

The place of understanding of the association but did no longer salve Flo's pain, because in truth she did now not need this marriage. Aunt Mai modified into her favored aunt. It seemed simply days inside the past that Flo had hidden in a fabric cupboard, guffawing until her elements harm as Aunt Mai regarded and looked for her. Was Aunt Mai irritated? Of course no longer. She concept it changed into a scrumptious funny tale. Now dour Uncle

Sam should deprive Flo of her aunt's hobby. This Flo brooded over as she rode to the church in a carriage with sister Parthe, Papa, Uncle Sam and the clergyman. Of direction Flo thought she ought to have been within the top notch bride's carriage with Aunt Mai. This separation end up only the start.

The wedding became a nightmare after Flo entered the church. Aunt Mai and Uncle Sam have been kneeling at the altar. Suddenly Flo felt her mom's sturdy hand on her shoulder. Flo felt herself being pulled lower returned into one of the first pews. Heavens! Had she genuinely kneeled amongst Aunt Mai and Uncle Sam? She couldn't don't forget doing it. But she want to have.

Mama's eyes have been giant after the rite. "Flo, what could you've got been questioning?"

Papa defended her. "The high-priced toddler have grow to be stressed."

Sister Parthe shook her head. "How mortifying."

Several days later Flo recorded the amazing event in her magazine:

On Wednesday Aunt Mai come to be married to Uncle Sam. I, Papa, Uncle Sam, Pop and Mr. Bagshaw (the clergyman) went first. Mama and Aunt Mai in the bride's carriage. Aunt Julia and Miss Bagshaw got here final. When they have been married we were all kneeling on our knees except Mr. Bagshaw. Papa took Aunt Mai's hand and gave it to Uncle Sam. We all cried except Uncle Sam, Mr. Bagshaw and Papa.[1]

There became absolutely no want to record her embarrassing attempt to hold the 2 participants aside! Though exceptional seven years antique Flo had one-of-a-kind nightmarish moments in her past. Strange matters had haunted her earliest years. Something had worried her very plenty. In truth a few component had seemed inner her. She had concept herself 'possessed'. But wherein had Flo acquired such an insane perception? She might also need to do not forget no fairy story or Bible tale that could plant such an idea. She clearly couldn't keep in mind. She feared being located out. She avoided everyone, throwing tantrums if asked to do something in the presence of others. At instances she had fought to stay inside the nursery in area of attend meals.

"But praise God I grew out of it, one manner or the other..." she remembered.

Social etiquette the various top class of England became so complex, so stressful, so troubling to the very more youthful. Flo had as soon as known as a duchess 'your grace', notable to be scolded later that she mustn't because of the fact Flo was of the 'gentry'. Then she once known as a baron through using the usage of that very discover, brilliant to be reprimanded that she mustn't because a baron is known as 'Lord', however his instant superior, a viscount, sincerely should be referred to as simply that - a viscount! And but the fears – if no longer the soreness - had nearly lengthy beyond away. At seven Flo did not fear social sports almost a lot. In fact she had even all started out to recognize the strain of better class English manners.

'Calling' changed into a awesome example. This became almost absolutely a girl's employer. If the Nightingales arrived in a positive city for a quick live Mama would possibly tour spherical to various homes of significance - never before one o'clock inside the afternoon of route - having the footman go away three calling cards at their doors. Her card changed into for the woman of the house, whereas Mr. Nightingale'sgambling gambling playing cards were for each the woman and the gentleman. The playing cards had been an invitation additionally. The recipient emerge as anticipated to go returned a card, or maybe a call. Sometimes the cardboard obtained at once results, with Mama and daughters invited into the drawing room. But even then, the call grow to be to final no more than 15 mins. And verbal exchange have become to be so bland as to broach not some thing extra vital than climate. Later, by way of mutual hobby, acquaintanceships might be cautiously increased. If a friendship advanced, the decision can also get nearer and towards the supper hour, ultimately assuming an invite to dine. When humans of the Nightingales' social popularity left town their footman took gambling cards spherical to all friends formalizing that fact.

"Once one learns the guidelines," rationalized Flo, "one in no manner is at a loss as to what to do."

The social abilties of Mama and Parthe have been exemplary. Parthe changed into high-quality three hundred and sixty five days older than Flo however had always laughed with out troubles via dinners and parties and paying visits. Perhaps Mama did no longer snigger so gaily as Parthe but she worked gently via social obligations though. So Flo persisted society, even dropping her fear. But if more youthful Flo misplaced her worry of socializing she did now not benefit peace of mind. Flo changed into confused. She did now not yet keep in thoughts that an soreness. As a baby knowledgeable via way of governesses stimulated through the fact that the outstanding poet George Herbert had lived a scant 15 miles or so from the Nightingales' Embley Park belongings she grow to be very familiar with Herbert's poem 'Pulley':

When God on the begin made man,

Having a pitcher of benefits status via,

"Let us," stated He, "pour on all we're able to:

Let the arena's riches, which dispersed lie,

Contract right into a span."

So strength first made a way;

Then splendor flowed, then know-how, honor, pride:

When nearly all become out, God made a stay,

Perceiving that on my own of all his treasure

Rest within the backside lay.

"For if I must," said He,

"Bestow this jewel also on my creature,

He could in all likelihood adore my gadgets in preference to me,

And relaxation in nature, no longer the God of nature;

So each want to losers be.

Yet permit him preserve the relaxation,

But hold them with repining restlessness:

Let him be wealthy and weary, that at the least,

If goodness lead him now not, yet weariness

May toss him to my breast."[2]

Herbert's poem changed into so actual to Flo. For she turn out to be very careworn. And she emerge as attracted to God. Her restlessness have turn out to be no longer glad with the aid of definitely retaining on the flow as Mama did. Mama have end up best at maintaining at the pass. Papa became not. He have become no longer with the Nightingale entourage even as quickly after the wedding Mama, daughters and servants left the Nightingales' summer domestic Lea Hurst in Derbyshire near Tapton. September have become the time of yr they journeyed south to their iciness domestic Embley Park in Hampshire. Their route couldn't were greater numerous. Mama did not plan the damaged axle that waylaid their awesome carriage as speedy as but the incident just appeared a part of her eccentric itinerary. Flo recorded each incident in her magazine.

In Staffordshire they were guests several days at Betley Hall. Flo and Parthe had the privilege of socializing with 12-one year-antique Miss Caroline, who changed into so gracious she pretended they were sisters. The Nightingale sisters had been in awe of Caroline's large doll, with its very non-public canopied bed and dresser beside her very own bed and cloth cupboard. On the grounds Caroline confirmed them a manner to shake inedible nuts from the superb spreading crown of a horse chestnut. Then Caroline's older brother took them rowing on a lake.

But inside the destiny Caroline located every day come to be no longer sunny at Betley Hall. "Georgiana, considered one in every of my older sisters, as soon as reduce her arm and it became inflamed..."

"Blood poisoning!" gasped Flo. For a few motive illness involved her.

"Georgiana hid the reality from mother," persisted Caroline. "She didn't need to jeopardize her piano classes. She loved her music."

"Oh, pray tell us what happened subsequent, Miss Caroline," stated Flo breathlessly.

"Her arm needed to be amputated."

Flo come to be chilled. The Nightingale ladies had visible little of infection and dying. Flo had no reminiscence of Grandpapa Shore loss of life on the same time as she becomeyears vintage. And whilst Flo subsequently met the melancholy Georgiana she knew she couldn't quickly overlook Georgiana's silly act. The foolishness of Georgiana ought to hold-out her. The terrible soul. That which Georgiana maximum desired have become lost to her forever because of her secrecy.

Mama and the women next had been web site traffic at Castle Downton. Here Flo encountered a modern surprise: a bath with taps. However her French maid Agathe spoiled the instantaneous through turning on a tap and in a few way jamming it simply so water flooded their room! After that disaster Flo broke down one of the beds by using leaping on it. It took all of Mama's social skills to easy over their barbaric get proper of access to. Boultibooke changed into their subsequent prevent. There Flo changed into greatly surprised thru Sir Harford Brydges at the same time as he spoke to her really as despite the fact that she had been an grownup. This have come to be doubly ironic whilst one in all her the the front enamel came out.

They next stopped in Herefordshire on the ruins of the 12th-century Goodrich Castle. Up inside the heights it received many web page visitors, in spite of the fact that the stone floors have been shot whole of thistles. The arched gateway changed into nevertheless intact as have been a number of the walls with their loopholes for firing weapons. All throughout the castle had been white wildflowers called "Travelers' Joy". Blackberries have been there too and yet again silly Agathe outstanding herself with the useful resource of ingesting such numerous she have come to be sick. Flo had to marvel how long Mama may want to tolerate the younger French maid's horrible judgment. This day Mama shrugged it off due to the fact she modified into reason on telling her daughters a tale. At this very fortress the famous poet William Wordsworth — however very a whole lot alive at 57 in 18- had the incident which have become the problem of his poem 'We are Seven'[3]:

I met a chunk cottage girl:

She modified into eight years vintage, she stated;

Her hair end up thick with many a curl

That clustered spherical her head.

The gist of Wordsworth's poem - which Mama recited to Flo and Parthe - modified into that the little woman insisted of her brothers and sisters, 'Seven boys and women are we,' despite the fact that Wordsworth - because of the reality he knewhave been lifeless and buried – argued:

"But they'll be dead; thoseare useless!

Their spirits are in heaven!"

'Twas throwing terms away; for nevertheless

The little maid might have her will,

And stated, "Nay, we are seven!"

Flo commenced out to surprise if each spot in Britain modified into like Goodrich Castle, a website of thought for some poet or novelist. Next Mama led the vacationers into Wales to find out Tintern Abbey, each specific ruin. First Flo changed into proven the mundane, just like the hollow thru which a cook dinner dinner exceeded meals to monks or similar to the big prayer room now floored with grass. Wordsworth had been right here too and Mama recited his poem 'Tintern Abbey'. His verses stuck flawlessly the effect of its rugged solitude and his rapture with nature, which changed into sincerely divine.

But Flo had to surprise why grownups had been so reluctant to speak of God. Why did they generally allude to God, in region of speak his holy names? Flo had noticed this currently. Outside of the church carrier God turned into now not frequently noted. Oh, the bad human beings within the village had been possibly to talk directly of God. But the well-to-do, the effective girls and gents, not often spoke like that. It appeared a signal of exceptional breeding that one did not factor out God. But why turn out to be this?

Mama, the ladies and their retinue of servants traveled through carriage at once to Monmouth, then via boat on the River Wye to Chepstow. Again they visited a fortress, Flo now so bored with ruins that she short forgot its name. From there they departed Wales on a steamship that plied the Severn River, with their massive carriage aboard too. At Bristol they disembarked and had to attempt seven inns in advance than they determined one appropriate. Flo carefully stated the range in her magazine. After Bristol they rolled directly to Bath, the fashionable hotel.

"With crescent-common streets," determined Flo.

Aunt Julia have become already in Bath, having lengthy beyond without delay there from the marriage. She have become there to study the way a certain home for elderly girls operated. Aunt Julia sensed the women have been uninterested in history and literature, so she attempted to entertain them, fun them with memories and allowing them to play with a dog. Yet Flo couldn't quite heat to her. Papa widely known Aunt Julia. Flo's high-priced cousin Hilary Carter counted Aunt Julia her preferred aunt, emphasizing how tough Julia tried to be 'pinnacle' and the manner tough she and the other spinster aunt Patty labored to attend to Grandpapa and Grandmama Smith. But even Hilary and Papa could not convince Flo to absolutely love her. After all, reasoned Flo, if Aunt Julia surely cared for the elderly Smiths in a ways-off Essex, then why changed into she constantly some place else?

Flo have become even unmoved with the aid of Aunt Julia's vintage cartoon of the 2 Nightingale daughters toddling beside their tall, lanky father on a walk. Aunt Julia confided to Flo, "You see how your sister Parthe clung to your Papa's hand at the same time as you - despite the fact that greater more youthful by means of way of using 365 days - stumped alongside thru the usage of your self!" Aunt Julia loved independence. So did Flo. And however Flo masses desired Aunt Mai. Perhaps Flo's indifference to Aunt Julia modified into due to the singular intensity of Aunt Julia's pastimes, the hawkeyed earnestness of Aunt Julia's ladies buddies. Or maybe Flo's questioning were encouraged with the resource of nasty remarks – not from Papa of course - she had overheard about women with 'advanced perspectives'. For a few factor reasons, to seven-12 months-vintage Flo Aunt Julia and her ladies friends were a humorless, colorless bunch.

After Bath, Mama, the women and their entourage trundled throughout 50 miles of forests and meadows to Embley Park, their wintry climate property in Hampshire close to Romsey.